GRAND FINISHES FOR

Carpentry

Also by Matt Nikitas

Grand Finishes for Walls and Floors

GRAND FINISHES FOR

Carpentry

A Step-by-Step Guide Through Molding Installation Projects

Matt Nikitas

Illustrations by Amy Evans and Matt Nikitas

Inside Photos by David Velez Felix

ST. MARTIN'S GRIFFIN 🅜 NEW YORK

www.stmartins.com

Illustrations by Amy Evans and Matt Nikitas
Interior photos by David Velez Felix
Used with permission

Book design by Jessica Shatan

Library of Congress Cataloging-in-Publication Data
Nikitas, Matt.
   Grand finishes for carpentry : a step-by-step guide through molding installation projects / by Matt Nikitas ; illustrations by Amy Evans and Matt Nikitas ; interior photographs by David Velez Felix.
      p. cm.
   Includes index.
   ISBN 0-312-26331-7
   1. Trim carpentry—Amateurs' manuals. 2. Finish carpentry—Amateurs' manuals. I. Title.
TH5695 .N55 2000
694—dc21   00-030735

First Edition: October 2000

10 9 8 7 6 5 4 3 2 1

This book is dedicated to

Cleo Barrett

(my mom)

who always said that

if you want something done right

then you've got to do it yourself

and

you can have fun doing it.

CONTENTS

With special thanks to

Alison Lazarus, Ron Chisenhall, Amy Evans, Christus Nikitas, Brian Leahy, David Velez Felix, Kathy Nikitas, Dan Waters, Charlie Spicer, Mike Nikitas, Joe Cleemann, Patsy Wiegelman, Devlin and Hot Dog; Humphrey, Kitty, and Brian; and to all my past and present clients in New York and California, including the Sackmans, Ernie and Kelly Anastos, the Feldermans, and Jon, Michelle, and Amanda Blieberg, whose faith and confidence in my work make me eternally grateful . . .

and especially to Hampton Coley.

GRAND FINISHES FOR

Carpentry

History of Moldings

MOLDINGS HAVE BEEN AROUND SINCE CIVI-lization began . . . though not always made out of wood. The ancient Greeks and Romans had masons that would create molds for various profile styles. They did this to duplicate the profile in stone and then add it to buildings, on both the inside and out. These might be used for private homes, though generally homes of the very wealthy . . . no one else could afford such craftsmanship.

The word first appeared in the English language in 1643 as *moulding*, which meant "an architectural ornamentation." These "mouldings" were still cast of stone (the ornamentation that was chiseled from stone was not technically a moulding) and basically for palaces, churches, and the very, very, *very* rich.

Walls were made of stone and brick pretty

much through to the 12th and 13th centuries. Because of weight and building dynamics, the ceilings, however, were almost always fashioned from some kind of wood. Even though crown moldings were seen in the Greco-Roman period, they really didn't start to gain popularity in

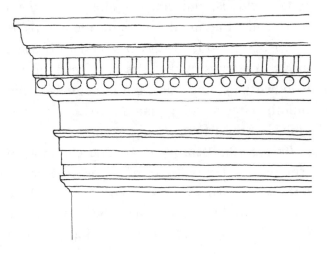

Europe until the turn of the millennium. Along the beams in the ceiling, or at the edge where it met the wall; at the bottom of a fireplace surround, or around a doorway or display case: moldings in wood started to appear everywhere to enhance and offer ornamentation to a space. Slowly man realized that wood was lightweight, durable, and made a good insulator. And because it was so plentiful, builders within societies began to incorporate it more and more in the construction of their dwellings.

Where Did Carpentry Come From . . . and Where Is It Now?

WORKING WITH YOUR HANDS, AND I'M sure no one will argue, is calming and cathartic. And people have always loved to work with wood. In the year 1378 the English finally spoke a word to describe the craftsman who worked with wood: the word *carpentry* was derived from the verb *carp,* which means "to cut."

In the 17th and 18th centuries carpenters made all the moldings to be installed by hand. They carried their tools—planes (called molding planes: much larger than ones commonly used today), chisels, and gouges—along with them and made the moldings right there on-site. Some of the wider pieces of wood to become crown moldings might have been made in the woodworking shop where the apprentices would pull the large molding planes across the planks, guided by the artisan *(head carpenter).*

By the 18th century it became common to trim out a home . . . to hide the uneven or unfinished corners left after construction. Base molding would trim out where the walls met the floor and door, and window casing trimmed

where these openings *opened* at the wall. This trim work is also called millwork or joinery.

Planing machines were invented in America around 1828 and at last adapted to molding

The Voice of Experience

I may be exaggerating, but it seems that *everyone* I've ever met who is a carpenter has pretty much possessed the same qualities: they have been creative, quiet, intelligent, and kind. Really! Jesus was a carpenter! I mean, how much kinder can you get? A guy named Ron who worked for me for two years in California as a carpenter was all those things. He was methodical and an excellent craftsman. He was a sweet guy who got along with my workers and clients. He read the *New York Times* (even though he lived in San Francisco). Heck, he even had long hair and a goatee (looked like Jesus).

manufacturing during the 1840s. By the mid-1800s this machinery was powered by water and steam and allowed moldings to be made quickly in the mills.

Now they were available to all. By the beginning of the 20th century it became standard building practice to finish all construction, both residential and commercial, with trim. The rich still had their homes decorated ornately with moldings. Yet even the simplest of places were starting to be trimmed out nicely.

TODAY IN CONSTRUCTION THERE ARE THREE TYPES OF carpenters: framers, millworkers, and interior finishers. The framer, or rough carpenter, is responsible for the skeleton, or frame, of the house. The millworker *makes* the doors and door frames, windows and window frames, and interior trim. Lastly, the interior finisher does just what you think. He/she installs cabinetry, constructs and installs the stairs and installs doors, and installs paneling and trim. And that portion of his/her duties is what we're concentrating on in this book.

Durability of Wood

WOOD IS A LIVING, BREATHING THING. (At least it is when part of a tree!) Even after it is milled from a felled tree, it still *breathes* somewhat. Though it is constantly drying after being processed, moisture is still absorbed and evaporated from it on a continual basis as it passes through the seasons. This means the wood is *hydroscopic*. Ever notice how the door sticks in the early spring but is fine once summer comes around? It is continually expanding and contracting, though no serious shrinkage occurs.

If you look at wood under a microscope you'll see a sort of honeycomb comprised of cavities of various shapes and sizes. This vast support system offers visible proof as to its strength, resilience, and durability.

Contrary to popular belief, wood does not decay naturally from *age*. It really can last *forever*. Wood decay is caused by one thing and *only one thing:* a wood-destroying fungi or mold, which is actually another form of plant life, albeit a real low one. This fungi can start in on a tree when still alive, though generally it invades

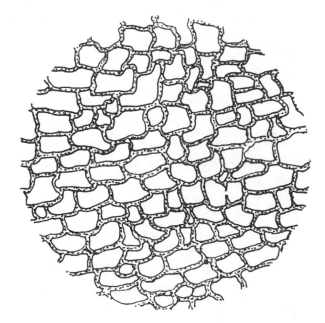

The honeycomb structure of wood as seen under a microscope.

the wood once dead. Obviously this fungi is very effective . . . take a walk through the woods in Yosemite National Park and see the various stages of decay everywhere among the new growth. Trees still standing, rotting slowly over time from this plant . . . trunks felled across the

forest floor. The last time I went backpacking there I was fascinated by the visible stages of the wood as this fungi eventually turns it into dirt. This rich new earth then aids the new trees to start up.

In your own home, when you see mold or stains . . . that is the fungus at work. It grows and thrives in dampness. However, if wood is completely submerged in water or exists in a completely dry situation, then it will last forever . . . well, a *really* long time. This fungi needs moisture. While a tunnel was being dug out in Washington, a log was found. One of the foremen was intrigued enough by the look of it to send it to a lab for identification. It turned out to be an extinct species of sequoia that existed on this planet 12 million years ago! And a portion of a sunken Roman houseboat was discovered at the bottom of Lake Nemi. It was over 2,000 years old yet was in good enough shape to be identified as coming from a spruce tree.

Hardwoods and Softwoods

THERE ARE TWO CLASSIFICATIONS OF TREES. There are hardwood, or deciduous trees . . . these are the broad-leafed trees that tend to lose their leaves in the fall. Then there are softwood, or coniferous trees. You got it: trees with cones or, more commonly, needles that stay on the tree year-round. Hardwoods tend to be harder (obviously) and heavier and, oddly enough, usually shrink more than softwoods.

HARD	SOFT
Mahogany	*Cedar*
Birch	*Pine, White*
Oak, White or Red	*Fir, Douglas*
Maple	*Redwood*
Ash	
Walnut	
Poplar	

Both hard and soft can be enjoyable to work with, though softwoods are much easier, especially for the beginner. Hardwoods, though, will be more resilient to denting. Softwoods are easy to nail: hardwoods usually require that you drill a pilot hole ahead in order to get the nail through.

I don't want to forget about **MDF,** which we on the job site called *the fake stuff.* It stands for Medium Density Fiberboard, and it's *very* dense. Today many moldings are available in it. It's heavier than a pine or poplar and though you can usually get a nail through with a nail gun, it's not as easy as softwoods to nail by hand (hammer). But it is a consistent material and the nails generally go straight where you drive them (when you hit a nail into a "real" wood it sometimes travels with the grain or knot and can bend to the side). MDF is never warped, and it's usually a lot less expensive than real woods.

The Voice of Experience

Choice cut of the tree: Only 25% of the tree can be used to create moldings and solid (non-veneer) furniture. The rest, though, is harvested for particleboard, plywoods, and MDF.

When we were building cabinets, I didn't mind working with MDF, although the dust particles are very small. With woods, usually a dust mask will sufficiently protect your lungs

The Voice of Experience

GO, HARDWOODS! I would certainly not discourage you from working with hardwoods. Generally, though, they are far more expensive than softwoods and appropriate for very high quality finish jobs that will end in the wood being finished with a stain and/or clear coating. When finishing a softwood project by painting it, you can correct any mistakes or overcuts with unlimited filling and caulking, so that when it's completely finished it'll look great. You don't have that luxury with hardwoods . . . each inside and outside corner must be done to perfection the first time, because wood fill and caulk (when used to fill gaps) will show after finished (polyurethaned). In this book I'm going to focus on the softwoods that are readily available at the lumber store and used in more than 90% of finish carpentry jobs: pine, poplar, cedar, and fir (and redwood, if you live in the western coastal states).

from airborne stuff while you're working. But MDF is made from a procedure of gluing together wood scrap (like particleboard but a much higher quality), and the resins that are used made me sufficiently concerned so that we always donned respirators when sanding, cutting, or sweeping. And though the cost was low, because MDF is so heavy and not easy to nail I tried to avoid using it for molding installations unless for some strange reason a client insisted on it.

A Carpenter's Basic Toolbox

THERE ARE *LOTS* OF TOOLS OUT THERE, BOTH regular and power-operated. I'm going to stick to the basics here and give you a primer on what will be useful for the majority of woodworking and especially for the projects in this book.

Starting with: get yourself a couple of *carpenter's* **pencils.** They are nice and fat so are easy to keep track of, the point won't break as easily as that of a school-issued #2, and they're easy to sharpen with a **utility knife,** when needed.

Sharpen your carpenter's pencil with the utility knife.

Utility knife and replacement blades

Like a pencil, a utility knife is a good tool for marking and scribing for cuts. Often I grab this out of the left pocket of my tool belt to shave a tiny area of molding that needed a little attention at the miter to get that joint to fit snugly. Another obvious aid is the **stepladder** for the crown, picture molding, or window casing project. I could almost always be guaranteed success with a 2' and a 4' one on hand.

If you have a basic **claw hammer**, you will be just fine. They are the hammer of choice and

The Voice of Experience

Don't use a *pen* or *marker* for your projects. Get into the habit of always using a pencil on any jobs around the house for marking both your molding and studs on the wall. Ink from pens and markers is *very* difficult to cover and will bleed through latex and even oil-based paints when you do your finish work. You can put on six coats of paint and a pen marking, on either the molding or the wall, will still bleed through. On our job sites we were always cursing the electrician, who was notorious for leaving his pen scribblings on the wall to note possible locations of new outlet receptacles or just to remind himself of some total. The only way to paint over ink is to prime it with shellac first. Shellac has an alcohol base and is smelly and bothersome to work with.

most widely used for most finish jobs. The **ripping hammer** is also lightweight and about the same size, with the claw sticking straight out, and, I find, more useful when the need arises to remove a nail. The **framing hammer** has the same design but is much larger. Though it is not intended for finish carpenters, I have to say that I prefer a smooth-faced framing hammer when installing moldings: it's a little heavier and packs a punch . . . it'll send those 2″ nails in quicker than a claw hammer will.

A nice **ripping bar** is a useful contribution to your toolbox. It can be used to pry out nails and help you get leverage to remove old moldings or a newly set piece that you may need to *tweak* a bit. However, a smaller pry bar (sometimes

The Voice of Experience

HAMMERHEAD Whatever one you feel most comfortable with, get yourself a high-quality one (price will probably tell you). There are $5 hammers available, and they are *worth* just that. I have used them and more than once struck one on something only to have the head crack and fly off. Besides being the end of that hammer, it also presented a dangerous situation (I wasn't hurt but could have been).

4- and 2-foot stepladders

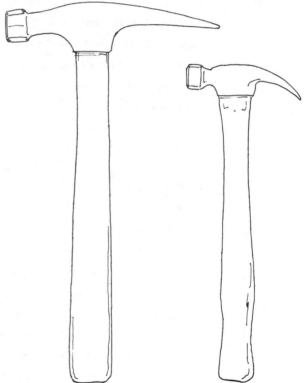

Framing hammer and claw hammer

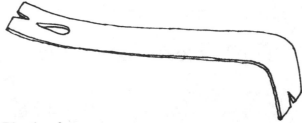

Ripping bar

Small pry bar, or "cat's paw"

called a **cat's-paw**) should be good enough for most molding jobs; it's nice and lightweight and fits well in both a toolbox and most toolbelts.

There are all kinds of **planes** out there, all created and adapted over the years to tackle a specific need for the carpenter. There are electric planes . . . noisy yet easy, they are handy for larger jobs where a lot of shaving may be called for and time is of the essence. There is the spokeshave, or the butterfly plane, which specializes in smoothing curved edges and most work in creating molded edges, like stopped chamfers, for instance. If your resources are somewhat unlimited, I would be the first one to encourage you to load yourself up with as many different planes as possible. The most common would be the bench plane. They come in all sizes, from the jointer plane (about 24") or the jack plane (14") to the smaller block plane (4–7"). There is the bullnose rabbet plane, which enables users to get flush with an inside corner of their work. I love my jack plane and use it when shaving down doors for perfect fits.

However, thinking back to how often we've used certain planes over the last 10 years, coupled with the needs for the specific projects in this book, I believe that if you have yourself a good **block plane** you'll be all set. They are smaller and more versatile than the rest and the ones that definitely get taken on the molding installation jobs. You can get one for as cheap as $14 or spend $160 (you don't need one this expensive unless you really want it).

First, block planes are separated into two main categories, depending upon the angle at which the iron (blade) sits in the body. The lowest angle is about 12 degrees; the other, more common angle is about 21 degrees. Though the low-angle plane is better for fine-tuning the end grain of moldings (say a mitered corner, for instance), you will get more use out of a standard-angle plane. As long as you keep the iron sharp and keep the plane square and fitted, it will be fine for shaving the end grain. Consider spending about $30 and getting one with an adjustable-throat (the slot at the bottom that allows the blade/iron to come through for shaving). This way, you'll have (almost) the best of both worlds. You'll be able to bring the iron in for fine-shaving an end of molding that will butt up against a door. Or adjust the

Pictured here are various-sized block planes.

iron out for a coarser shave: when you encounter a curved floor and want to contour the bottom of your base to lessen a gap showing, for instance.

Another tool that will come in handy (and I have seen one in the bottom of practically every tradesman's toolbox) is the **drywall grate.** They look like a combination plane-cheese grater and come in various sizes. One the size of a small block plane will come in handy when working around drywall: shaving edges of walls or corners that bulge out strangely.

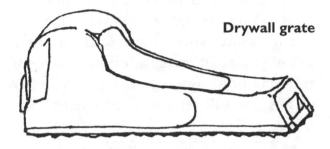

Drywall grate

The **chisels** are probably the most recognized carpenter's aid, second only to the hammer. They consist of the blade, handle, and tang. Because they are struck with a hammer or mallet on the top of the handle, a high-quality chisel will have blade and tang forged out of one piece of steel. You can get a decent set of three for around $25, which is not a bad place to start.

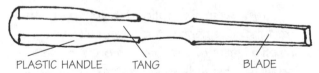

PLASTIC HANDLE   TANG   BLADE

Cross-section of a chisel showing the blade, tang, and handle as one piece of forged steel

You can spend $50 for a set of chisels or even $30 for one. The determining factor really should be: *will you take care of them?* You can keep them sharpened with either an **oilstone** or

a **waterstone.** One requires a light lubrication of a sharpening oil to prevent the surface from becoming clogged with metal particles (and thus marring the edge of your blade) and the other requires a light coating of water. Lay the blade or iron (from your plane) with the cutting edge down first on the rougher stone and move it in a figure-eight motion to hone (sharpen) the edge. Then follow by turning the blade over and smoothing it back and forth a few times to remove any burr. Follow with the finer grit stone. You can usually get one stone that has two sides, one with the coarse side (about 800 grit) and the other a bit finer (around 1500–2000 grit). This should be fine for your basic-taking-care-of tools . . . a carpenter will usually have a third stone with the finest grit of about 6000 to finish maintaining his chisels and irons with a polished finish.

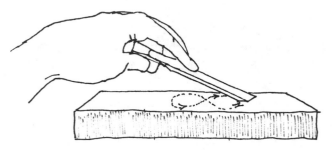

First place the blade or iron on the stone at an angle and hone in a "figure-8" motion. Turn over and repeat, with blade against the stone at less of an angle.

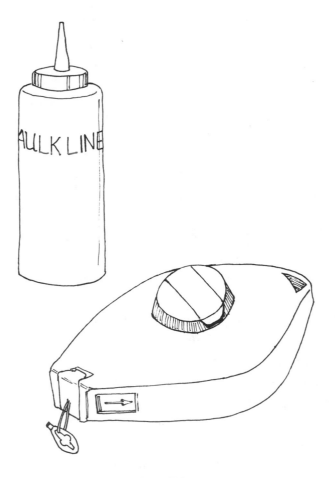

Chalk line reel and re-fill

Even if you get a waterstone, it would not hurt to have a small container of lubricating or **machine oil** in your toolbox. If you dip each nail in it before driving into the molding, the greased nails will greatly reduce the chances of splitting the wood (but I'll go into that in more detail later).

The **chalk line reel** is another marking tool that, though not essential, is usually found in a carpenter's toolbox. A line, along with some re-fill colored chalk, can be had for around $10. I will show how it can help in situating the crown molding in the right place for installation.

A few other basics are the **caulking gun,** a pair of **pliers** (either regular or end cutters, for removing nails), **wood glue**, a pair of **safety glasses**, the **nail set** (there are different size

The Voice of Experience

The metal clip on the edge of a tape measure tends to go out of whack to the tune of $1/16$" very easily. When going for a really *precise* measurement, and when I have a helper with me, I will generally measure off the 1" mark and add that inch at the end before making my mark. This may seem like splitting hairs to get the *exact* measurement, but it often saves us shaving off a length of crown one more time before installing. Obviously, to get that exact measurement, one person has to hold the tape on that 1" mark at one end of the molding while the other marks the molding where needed at the other end (you can't take lengthy accurate measurements by yourself).

heads for larger and smaller nails; sold in three-packs for around $10), **shims** (I usually go through one pack for one crown or one base installation . . . they cost a buck each and are made of cedar, pine, or redwood: it's always good to have extra around), and the retractable **tape measure.** For some reason, tape measures disappear on job sites more than *any* other tool, and so consequently I have eight of them in my garage (always a spare, and they make great gifts, too). You can invariably find a good 25' one for under $13 if you look . . . whenever I see them for under $10 I can't resist stocking up on a few more.

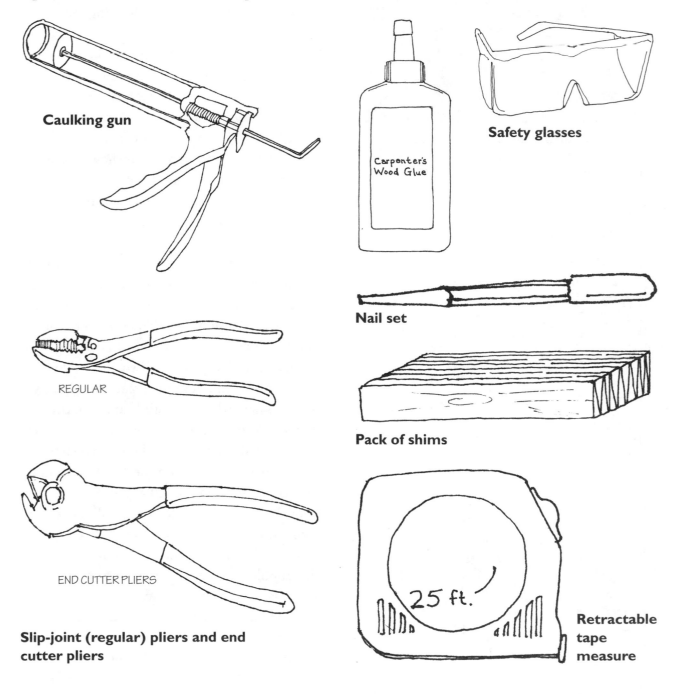

Caulking gun

Safety glasses

Nail set

REGULAR

Pack of shims

END CUTTER PLIERS

Slip-joint (regular) pliers and end cutter pliers

25 ft.

Retractable tape measure

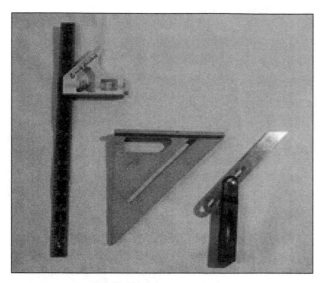

Combination square, try square, T-bevel

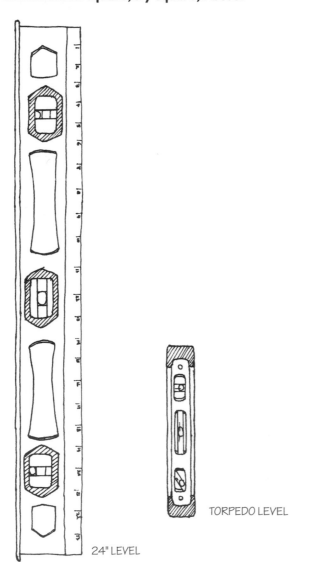

TORPEDO LEVEL

24" LEVEL

A carpenter uses several tools for the layout of a job and for marking pieces. For these projects, a **T-bevel** will come in handy if there is an odd angle where two walls meet and you need to determine that miter for the molding. The **combination square** (about $10) and the **try square** (about $8) will aid in flat-marking base molding pieces for cutting, as well as checking the square of your piece once cut.

And of course there's the **level.** The word *level* refers generally to straight horizontal lines while *plumb* describes a straight vertical line. They all have at least one little tube of colored liquid with a small air bubble inside that when settled in the center of the lines on the tube shows the levelness of the surface the level is placed on. A good carpenter's level will have several tubes situated in the tool that will show a level surface as well as a plumb one. Though most carpenters have a variety of lengths (48", 36", for example), a 24" length is versatile enough to have in your toolbox and will handle most interior finish carpentry projects. I also have a **torpedo level** which is about 8" long. It's light and can be set by itself on many a surface, large and small, to allow me to keep something level as I nail it in. You will need to know where the studs are and, coupled with the knowledge that they are almost certainly located every 16" in all walls an **electronic stud finder** will be your best bet in finding them. It runs for about $20 and is powered by a 9-volt battery. The better ones will show you, during use, when you encounter one edge of the stud and then indicate where the other edge is. This should give you a better idea of where the center is, helping you to avoid just missing it with the nail. Over the years I have heard even the best contractors curse when using electronic stud finders: they are *not* 100% dependable. But

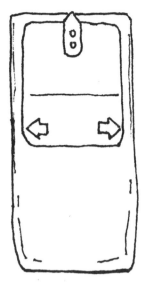

**Electronic
stud finder**

once you realize that there have been a lot of materials that make up many different kinds of walls over the years, whether lathe-and-plaster, drywall, or even a backer board, you probably will tend to be a bit more patient. Most stud finders operate by holding them on the wall still and simultaneously holding in the side button(s). Once the light goes out, then move the stud finder slowly along the surface. I find that I get many "false positives" . . . or, conversely, the light may not go on at all encountering a stud. With the 16" spacing for studs in mind I can usually figure out when I just need to lift the stud finder off the wall and set it back down and start again.

If you want to execute your molding installation without a power tool, a **hand-operated miter saw** should do the trick. The drawback would be a restriction of the *size* molding you can work on with this saw: most won't accommodate a base molding larger than 3½" or a crown molding wider than 2¾". Another downside to these is that because they are lightweight they will move around when in use unless bolted down to a bench or table.

The Voice of Experience

GIVE IT THE BLUE RIBBON Because I was a painting contractor before branching out with cabinetry and woodworking, I am a die-hard believer in **blue painter's tape.** Mainly, I use It to "mark" walls and floor where the studs are. It's more expensive than regular masking tape: goes for about $6 for a 1½" roll. There is less adhesive on the back of the tape than with regular masking tape. The first reason I use painter's tape is to limit the amount of priming/painting that will have to follow a molding installation (no marks on the wall or floor to have to re-touch). And when I remove it from the wall it's highly unlikely that any paint will come off with it (a mess that is time-consuming to correct because you have to spackle, sand, prime, and re-paint). Most masking tapes also leave a bit of glue or paper on the surface after removing, even after a short period of time. We can lay red paper down to protect a room or area where the work will happen and seal the edges with blue tape . . . walk over it for several days, and it still lifts off nice and clean.

Whether you use a power-operated saw or not, a couple of saws around will always find some use. A fine-toothed **backsaw** comes in handy for smooth cuts that might show. For the rough cuts there is a basic **rip** or **crosscut handsaw.** One of these at 16" could run you $25; however, since all saws are expensive to re-sharpen once dulled, get yourself a nice one for around $12. There is the dovetail and panel saw,

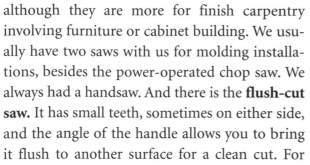

although they are more for finish carpentry involving furniture or cabinet building. We usually have two saws with us for molding installations, besides the power-operated chop saw. We always had a handsaw. And there is the **flush-cut saw.** It has small teeth, sometimes on either side, and the angle of the handle allows you to bring it flush to another surface for a clean cut. For instance, when you need a straight cut at the bottom of casing to allow for a new floor that's going in and the handle of any other saw would get in the way and prevent a straight cut.

You will need a **coping saw** (about $10) for all your coped joints on the crown and base molding. Have yourself a packet of extra blades on hand, too ($6).

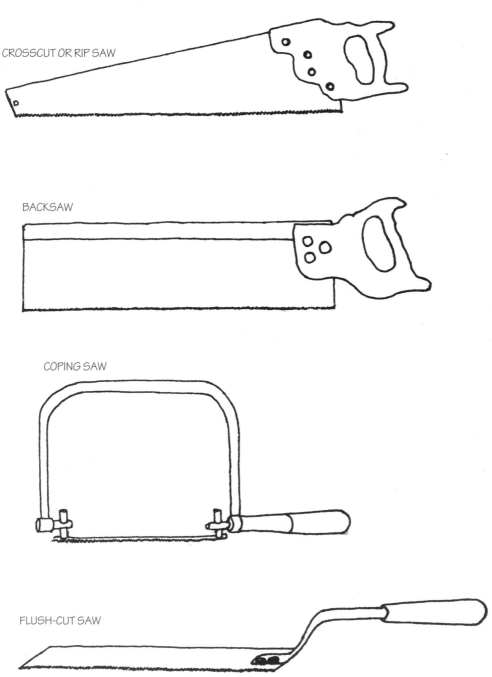

CROSSCUT OR RIP SAW

BACKSAW

COPING SAW

FLUSH-CUT SAW

For finishing, besides keeping a few pieces of **sandpaper** on hand (80–120 grit) and flexible **sanding blocks** there are the **files** and **rasps**. The rasp has the larger teeth for faster scraping/sanding and so leaves the wood surface rougher than the files. The file has smaller and more teeth and can offer a finer sand, though the file's teeth become clogged easily and so require frequent cleaning. Both come in many shapes and sizes. These are generally kept on hand by most finish carpenters. You can get a full set for under $10 that will have a variety of sizes that might be called for when fine-tuning the coped joints of the moldings. These include a flat and half-round rasp as well as various-shaped files: flat, half-round, round, and three-square.

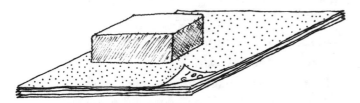

80 to 120 grit sandpaper sheets and flexible sanding block

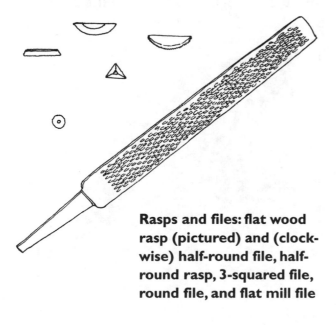

Rasps and files: flat wood rasp (pictured) and (clockwise) half-round file, half-round rasp, 3-squared file, round file, and flat mill file

Oh, and get yourself a good cloth **tool belt** (about $25). (They come more commonly in leather, but being that I'm a vegan I wouldn't suggest you go that route.) They are made for all types of contractors: drywall guys, framers, electricians. A carpenter's belt should hold nails, your hammer, a nail set, a pencil, and have a few extra pockets/compartments for the things you use constantly (like pliers and utility knife).

A good cloth tool belt enables the carpenter to carry his/her most-used tools.

Last, to store everything: a nice, big **5-gallon drum**. Once full of joint compound, a drum that has been cleaned and dried makes a great storage bucket. They have a handle that make them easy to carry. And cloth storage pocket/organizers (about $16) that fit around these tubs are made and sold specifically with carpenters in mind. The multiple pockets hang on both the inside and out of the bucket and ensure that each tool has its own home, preventing them from damaging each other . . . like when a chisel sits in the same place as a pound bag of nails, for instance. You can buy an empty drum, or if you know of a building site and/or a contractor, ask if there's a spare that you can have.

There is the traditional **toolbox,** however, made of either metal or plastic, and those can be good for storing the nails, screws, or other tools when not in use that won't damage or dull each other when stored together. One about 19" long x 9"deep x 9" tall may run you anywhere from $10 to $25 and is a good place to start. There are also tool *bags* out there now, with lots of pockets and compartments.

5-gallon bucket with organizer/pockets

Power Tools

THERE ARE PLENTY OF POWER TOOLS OUT there that go along with woodworking, like routers, planers, band saws, and electric sanders. For the projects in this book, though, you can get by with just a few. Everyone should have a **table saw,** really. You can start out with a decent table saw with a 10" blade for under $60. If you plan to use it often a good one can be had for around $130. (You can spend upward of $1,200, if you want to.) When I work on things in my garage, I like to set the saw on its stand (which can be purchased as an accessory or built out of 2x4s and plywood). However, when we cart table saws around to job sites they generally get placed on the floor (on top of a drop cloth) and we do all our cuts on it like that. For the wainscoting installation some lengthwise cuts may be called for (to trim down a piece that runs into a corner, for instance). A nice fine-finish blade will allow you to get a clean cut. However, it is not *necessary* . . . these cuts can be made with a little more effort by using a hand-saw or even the jigsaw.

I have never liked the name "jigsaw" (it sounds like a racial slur); companies now refer to it as an orbital saw, a bayonet saw . . . and a **saber saw**—and that's what we call it on the job site, even though "jigsaw" is still used. You can

Orbital saw

purchase a saber saw for $50, but I wouldn't advise it. The blades bend easily when in use and even break off from time to time. I got mine for about $150. It has four orbital settings (for hard, soft, and medium-density materials) and a chip blower that I can direct in different directions, and I can adjust the speed. The reason I bought it, though, was its blade. This saw calls for a longer than ordinary blade that is changed without tools. One end sits up inside the head (clamped into the "blade plunger"), and, most important, there is a groove in a roller guide on the foot plate that holds the other end of the blade in place. The blade stays in line and gives a straight, fast cut, and it *rarely* ever breaks.

The saber saw will come in handy for quick, small cuts, substitute for the table saw for long cuts, and is a necessity when cutting holes in the new wainscoting to accommodate switches and outlet receptacles. And in this book's projects it can do all the things that a table saw would.

You will find a **circular saw** on just about every commercial job site, from the framing to the finishing. Most homes have them, too . . . I was weather proofing a summer home out in East Hampton on Long Island, New York, and was surprised to even find one in *their* basement (this was not a power tool home). Circular saws are versatile, easy to use, and a good one, which you can get for about $150, will last almost forever. They are more mobile than the table saw and can be used for quick cuts and rip cuts. They are even better than a plane for shaving down a door that sticks. The most common circular saw has a 7¹/₄" blade. There are larger-motored saws fitted with the same size blades called worm drive or hypoid saws (I have this one). I also came across a neat little **4¹/₂" trim saw**, which is basically a smaller version of the 7¹/₄" circular saw.

Though the price tag was close to that of its larger cousin (about $140) I couldn't resist, as its lightweight compactness suggested ease of use.

7¹/₄" hypoid circular saw and 4¹/₂" trim saw

The Voice of Experience

COLORS OF THE WORLD (Rule of the Jungle): Though there aren't that many primary colors available out there, power tool companies are generally known for their own color. And you will *not* see two different tool companies with the same exact color . . . they seem to be very territorial about this. Ryobi: sky blue, Bosch: dark blue, Hitachi: green, Porter Cable: gray, Milwaukee: red. The glaring exception is that both Stanley and DeWalt use the scuba-diving yellow, although DeWalt makes primarily power tools while Stanley makes mostly hand tools and accessories.

Should You Invest in a Chop Saw? A Nail Gun?

A MITER SAW, OR "CHOP SAW," AS IT'S AFFEC-
tionately known on the job site, will be a
help to you when you install your new
moldings. You certainly will use it for base,
crown, picture molding installations, and many
other building projects later down the line. I got
my first one 14 years ago after visiting my
brother. He had just purchased one to aid in the
building of a fireplace mantel. After he showed it
off for a couple of cuts, I was hooked. The precision! The ease!

The arm (with the 10" blade) is stationary
and pulled down onto the piece of molding to
be cut, hence the term *chop*. One can be had for
under $200. There are big 12" blade saws out
there, capable of handling larger profiles of
molding. There are the more complex (and
expensive) slide compound miter saws (about
$500); also, their arms slide, which enables you
to cut even larger pieces of molding and at various angles . . . these are a must for molding
installations where the crown or base is over 4".

A chop saw is a good investment. In the early
eighties we had very few finish carpentry jobs,
and I would take care of most jobs with my
hand-operated miter box and table saw. This
miter saw ran me about $100. It was fine, yet
because I had to move the saw blade back and
forth manually to cut the wood my cuts weren't
always right on the money.

Miter saws will aid you immeasurably on
most projects. We drag ours (about 35 pounds)
around to job sites for just about any job that
calls for cutting wood: it's quick, easy, and precise. You can set it right on the floor for opera-
tion, although you should put a drop cloth
under it to avoid damage to the floor. If you have
a table or platform for it, a good companion tool
is the material stand that enables you to work
with long pieces of molding and still get accu-

Pictured here: 12-inch "chop saw"

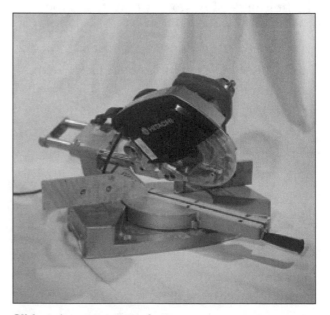

Slide miter compound saw

rate cuts. These stands are adjustable, lightweight, and might run you $20 and can also be used in conjunction with your table saw.

What about a **pneumatic nail gun?** Quite simply, they're definitely worth it if you're planning on a lot of carpentry projects, including molding installation throughout your house. A hose runs from the nail gun (nailer) to a compressor, which, with the buildup of pressure, gives the gun the power to shoot nails. A nail gun is very easy to operate and maintain. Keep it clean and pop a few drops of oil in the male end of the nailer before you attach the hose each time you decide to take it out for use. Loading the nail magazine is very straightforward and you can view the amount of nails left as you use

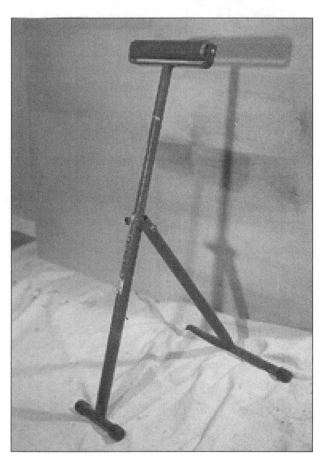

Material stand

The Voice of Experience

Check the chop saw for accuracy. If you do end up using a chop saw, it's a good idea to double-check the blade and make sure it sits squarely in the housing so your cuts will all be true. (This is especially true if you've rented one, as those are, like rented cars, not treated as well as owned ones.) Set your index point to zero and make a test cut, laying a scrap piece of wood (something square, like a 2x4, would be ideal) on the table against the fence. Check the cut piece with your try square. Ninety percent of the time when something is out of whack it's the index point that's floated. Move it slightly and continue to make test cuts, checking them until you get a true square. At this point you should be able to unscrew the index point (some call for an Allen or hex wrench) and carefully move it (without moving the table/blade) to 0. Now check again with a test cut until it's square.

Cut a piece at the zero-degree index and check it with your try square.

If adjustment is necessary, move index point.

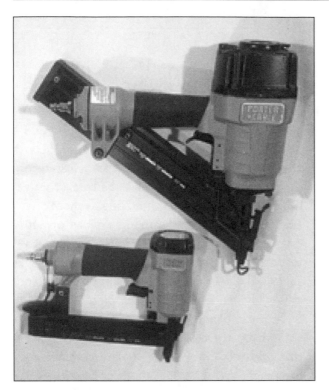

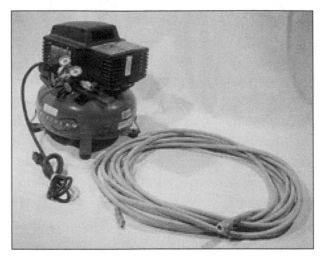

Pancake compressor and hose

When finished using at the end of the day, turn off, open valve, and rest on block to allow any moisture buildup to drain out.

2¹/₂" finish nailer and crown stapler

them. A high-quality angle finish nailer can be had for $200, one that will handle nails up to 2¹/₂".

The **compressor** is a simple machine . . . there are various sizes that suit them for different jobs. Unless you plan to have multiple hoses for a crew of framers, an ideal one for finish nailers (and for a home shop) is a 1 hp. pancake compressor with a PSI (Pounds per Square Inch) between 80 and 100. These are oilless (you don't have to add and keep track of the oil as you would with a larger compressor) and, like the nailer, are relatively easy to maintain. Each time you get ready for use, close the drain valve, plug it in, and turn it to the "auto/on" position. The motor goes on as pressure builds in the tank. Adjust the regulator: the jobs a finish carpenter will do suggest a setting of 100–120 PSI. The motor will stop when the tank is full. When

you're finished, turn the switch to "off," unplug the machine, and set it somewhere to allow the condensation to run out . . . outside is good. Rest it at an angle with the valve closest to the ground and open the drain valve. Leave it for a half an hour or so, to make sure that all the water comes out. It might run you about $150. The hose and fittings would be another $30. So figure with nails and tax that you'll have the setup for under $400.

You will then be one of the big boys (or girls). Your nail goes *exactly* where you want it to without any movement of your wood piece once the nailer is in place and then the nail is shot into place. And I've found that you're much less likely to split the wood when using a nailer. *And* it saves you an *incredible* amount of time. Think about it: rather than hammer in each nail and then follow by setting it with a nail set, you just *chu-ching* each nail in with one pull of the trigger . . . the nail is in place and set for you.

I have always been a holdout on the latest stuff, and I didn't even invest in a compressor/nailer setup until four years ago, and we did plenty of interior finish carpentry jobs before that. So I really think you can work fine without one: your job will just take a bit longer. If you want to try one out, chances are you can *rent* a compressor and nailer, along with the hose and fittings from a tool rental place for a total of about $45/day plus nails.

Safety

OF ALL THE TRADES, CARPENTRY HAS THE most potential for you to hurt yourself. The power tools, with sharp blades and quick action, demand constant attention and alertness. Even the non-powered tools have razor edges and chiseled points, and care with usage always has to be the priority.

Over the years I have heard so many stories about experienced tradesmen who lost a finger, toe, or eye (and worse) from a relaxed and unaware moment during work. Enough to *always* make sure that I'm awake and focused on what I'm doing. Whenever I turn on a circular saw I concentrate completely until it's turned off, no matter how simple the cut I've got to make. I *always* wear my safety glasses, even for driving in one nail by hand.

Anyway. Besides alertness, invest in a small, portable **first-aid kit** and always have it on hand near your tools. Keep it stocked: whenever you use any of the contents, replace them right away. I have an 11" x 7" metal one mounted in my shop that contains Band-Aids of all sizes, gauze, antiseptic wipes, bandages, an instant cold pack, cloth tape, first-aid cream, tweezers, Tylenol, and a first-aid guide. This one ran me about $30 and comes to the larger jobs we take on. But I also have a compact kit, about $4^1/_2$"x $5^1/_2$", that comes everywhere with me. It's also got Band-Aids, antiseptic wipes, tweezers, first-aid cream, and a fact-and-guide book for emergencies, and I got this one for about $8.

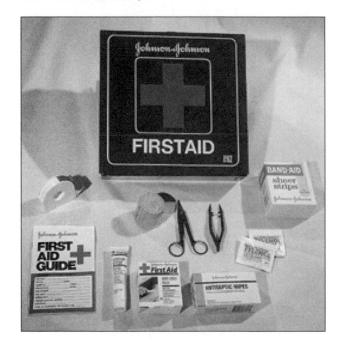

CHAPTER 1

Install a Base Molding

More History of Moldings

LIKE ALL MOLDINGS, THE BASE MOLDING originated in stone. Oddly enough, you wouldn't really see much base back in the Medieval days, when walls and floors were stone and brick. Even with all the ornate stuff around the ceiling paneling (which was traditionally wood), the floors were usually unadorned. It wasn't really until the 15th century during the Gothic period (when paneled walls became popular) that base molding was added. And it came about for the same reason that we use it today; beauty and (most important) function: it hides the irregular meeting of the floor and the wall, and it protects the walls when the floors are being cleaned (by brooms, mops, and, today, vacuums).

Choose a Molding (or Two, or Three)

HAVE YOU DECIDED WHAT KIND OF MOLDING you'd like to put down at the base? There are lots of styles to choose from. A lumber store that sells moldings should be able to provide you with their own molding profile book. You'll be able to see the variety of profiles as well as wood stocks that are available. The place that I frequented in San Francisco charged $3.50 for their catalog but credited that amount back when I purchased wood.

Base molding used to be exclusively made up of several pieces put together. It would consist of

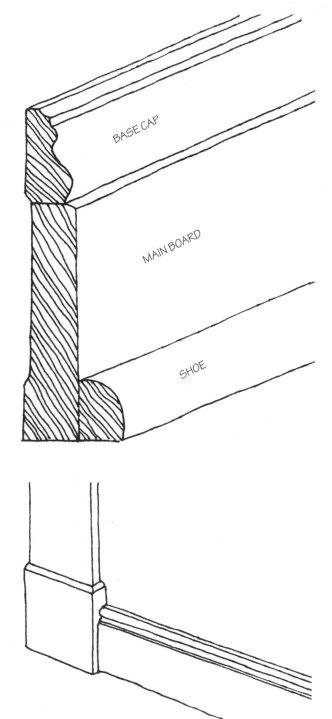

BASE CAP

MAIN BOARD

SHOE

Base molding butts up against door casing.

the main board, a base cap or crown, and sometimes a shoe molding. Today in the higher-ceilinged rooms it is still common to find a three-piece base. The nice thing about a multiple-piece base is that you can mix-and-match the base caps and shoes available with the main board and come up with a simple design to a very ornate one. And you can skip the shoe and concentrate on customizing your new base configured with a main board and a base cap. The installation for multiple- or single-piece is pretty much the same. (I'll illustrate the differences later on in this chapter.) Since there are some pretty nice moldings available that come in one piece, I'll focus this particular installation project on a one-piece molding, with guidance on how to continue on your own with a multiple-piece base.

Now at the planning stage is the time to decide whether to change/replace the door casing also. Since it runs vertically to the floor and

The Voice of Experience

If the base molding you chose is over 2½" tall, then you may end up with slight gaps between your new base and the floor. It's difficult to find an incredibly *flat* floor, especially in old homes. I'll show you how to plane down the bottom of a single-piece molding to get a better fit. Realize, though, that a shoe molding will bend and go with the contour of the floor. If a really clean sealed look is what you want at the floor, you might consider adding a shoe to your configuration.

the base butts up against it, it should be completed (chapter 4: "Install a Door or Window Casing") before the base installation. We have come across many a job where the client decided to replace the door casing at a later date. We would try to go with a like-casing for replacement. If the new profile was smaller, then there would be a portion of the base that would have to be mended, either with a piece of the base or, if locating that wasn't possible, then with wood filler. Doing the door casing before the base makes for cleaner joints and allows you to avoid any possibly messy mends like that.

Various profiles of one-piece base moldings, main boards, base caps, and shoe moldings

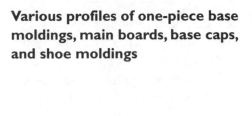

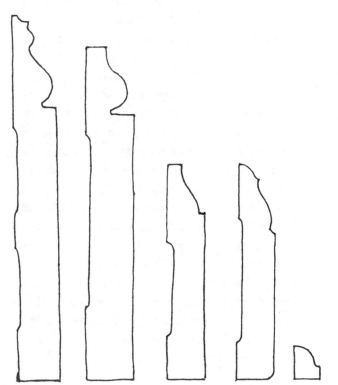

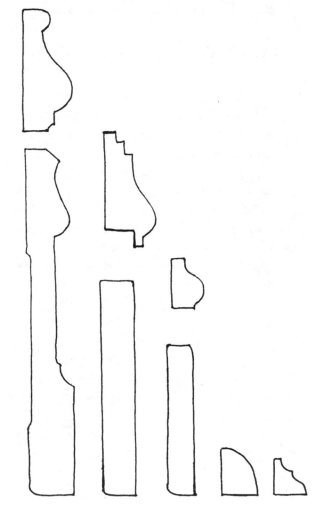

Assess How Much You'll Need and Purchase the Molding

MEASURE THE PERIMETER OF THE ROOM where you'll install the new base. Figure in extra: maybe 4 extra feet for a small (28') to medium-sized room (56') or add 6' for a larger room (74'). It's kind of like wallpaper in that you want to make sure you have plenty of material ready to go when you're there doing the job. You shouldn't have a problem returning extra uncut pieces, so the more you get as extra for safety, the better.

Let's assume that there is an old molding that will have to be removed first before you begin your new base installation.

The Voice of Experience

What lengths must you travel? Lumber stores get their moldings from the mills in 16' pieces. So you should almost always be able to get that length. The longer the pieces you start with, the less cutting. Sixteen feet is an awkward length, though. You really have to determine which length(s) will work best for you in your particular situation, taking into account: Do you have to go around tight bends to get the molding to the site (or is there a window you can pass them through)? Will the work space accommodate larger pieces? There are usually 12' and 10' lengths, which are fairly easy to work with in most situations. If you have four 11' walls, then it would make sense to get four 12' pieces. If you live in a big city, 8' lengths might be easier to carry down the street . . . you could even get into a cab with the ends of 8' lengths sticking out the window (with red tags on the ends).

The Voice of Experience

In the *old* days before drywall, the base molding was usually nailed directly into the wall studs before the wall was plastered. This actually served as a guide for plasterers to make sure their walls were flat. The base then would be partly buried; in other words, the wall surface would be *farther* out than the back of the molding (where it sat on the studs). If you are hoping to remove an old base molding that was installed in this fashion and replace it, the new base will have to be shimmed out to the level of the wall. When I've encountered this on a job, I first would determine the depth difference between the surface of the stud and the surface of the wall. Rather than use shims from a pack (because the shape is graded from a thick end to a thin end), I would use some form of inexpensive lattice molding, either $\frac{1}{4}$", $\frac{3}{8}$", or whatever the depth difference called for. If it was $\frac{1}{8}$" I would score and cut enough pieces from a single sheet of Luan plywood in that thickness. You only need one or two small nails to hold each in place on a stud, or you can staple them on.

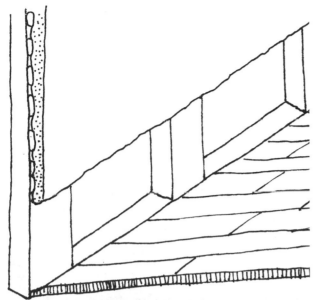

If old base molding had been installed directly onto studding, then install a lattice as a shim on each stud (the thickness of the plaster/drywall) so that the new base will sit flush to wall.

The Voice of Experience

Maybe you love the molding in your home, old, big, and beautiful as it is. Is there just one section that's damaged? Or did a recent renovation to a room leave a space on the wall with a poorly matched replica? There may be a more upscale lumber place nearby that specializes in duplicating that molding for you. There was one in San Francisco that would do just that. As long as you could bring in a small sample of it, they could re-calibrate the knives on their milling plane (done right on-site) for a fee of $75. This would duplicate the molding's profile, and then they could run off however much you needed.

Prepwork: Remove the Old Molding and Locate the Studs

MATERIALS CHECKLIST

- [ ] Claw or framing hammer
- [ ] Small pry bar
- [ ] Utility knife
- [ ] Stud finder
- [ ] Pencil
- [ ] Blue painter's tape
- [ ] End-cutter pliers
- [ ] Work gloves

STEP 1 *Break the seal where the old molding meets the wall.* Take your utility knife and score the top edge of the old base molding where it touches the wall. This will cut any seal between the molding and the wall, whether it be caulk or paint. This way, when you go to remove each piece you can avoid pulling paint, plaster, or the drywall's paper veneer off with it.

STEP 2 *Locate the studs.* Using your stud finder and pencil, go around the room to find and mark the studs. Each time you find one, mark it with a piece of blue painter's tape, about 8" up from the floor.

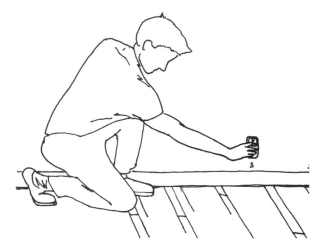

Locate the studs with a stud finder and mark lightly with a pencil. They should be found approximately 16 inches apart.

The Voice of Experience

My dad was very organized. When I was watching him at his workbench he always told me that he made sure to hammer or bend in any old nails sticking out of scrap pieces of wood. He would do this right away as he came upon or removed a piece for any project he was working on. He pointed out that he did this to avoid scratching his hands or arms (or, worse, stepping on one later on) when handling the scrap. And he did it immediately because he always had so many things on his mind (he was a state congressman, local anchor on TV, host of a radio talk show, publisher of a local newspaper, and sold insurance) and he would be apt to forget about the protruding nail if he didn't take care of it right away. This always made sense to me, and it doesn't take that much time, anyway. Yet I am always surprised at how many remodelers or construction guys won't do this, thus further demanding that they get their annual tetanus shot.

The Voice of Experience

PAY ATTENTION, PLEASE Utility knives are a toolbox must, though dangerous. I try to be careful and *(knock wood)* have yet to cut myself seriously with one on a job. However, last November when I was home putting a sheet of plastic "tile" in the upstairs bathroom of a dollhouse that I had put together for my two nieces, Zoe and Ali, I was getting a little anxious to get it finished and packed to send to them for Christmas and wasn't paying close enough attention, and as I was scoring the edge of the "tile" I ran the knife's blade through the side of my thumb. I didn't need stitches, *but it really hurt,* bled a *lot,* and I had to bandage it up quick and stop working for the night.

STEP 3 Now remove your old molding by tapping the pry bar behind the molding at a stud with your hammer. (If you set the pry bar

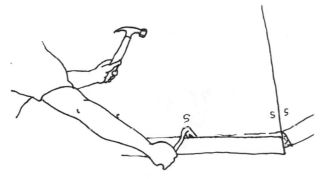

Remove the old base with hammer and pry bar.

between studs there won't be anything behind the wall to lever against, and you will probably punch a hole in the wall.)

STEP 4 Once you get all your old molding off the walls ready it for the trash. For carrying purposes, we would generally break or cut the pieces down to manageable 4' lengths and tie them with string. This size would be okay for the dump . . . if you want to include them in household trash you may have to make smaller (2') lengths . . . after, of course, checking with local ordinances as to what kind of building materials are allowed as household trash.

Cut and Install the Base Molding

MATERIALS CHECKLIST

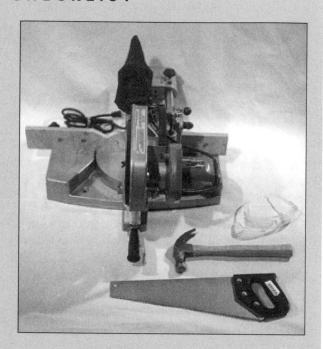

- Drop cloth
- Tape measure
- Pencil
- Coping saw
- Crosscut or backsaw
- Power chop saw
- 2" 6D or 2½" 8D finish nails
- Oil
- 1¼" 3D brads (nails)
- Nail set
- End-cutter pliers
- Half-round and three-square file
- Shims
- Safety glasses
- Utility knife
- Adjustable T-bevel (if your room has any corners other than 45 degrees)
- Try square or combination square
- Claw hammer

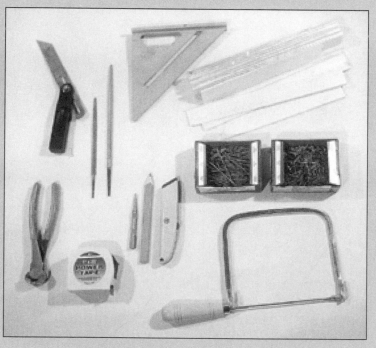

FIND YOURSELF A GOOD WORK AREA CLOSE TO (or in) the room to get the new molding. If you're worried about scratching wood floors, place a drop cloth under the molding if you're going to work on the floor. If you have the luxury of a worktable at or near where you're working, then even better. Just make sure that the saw is level and stable on the table.

There Are Five Kinds of Joints

THERE IS THE SIMPLE 90-DEGREE **BUTT JOINT.** This one is good for when the new base will die directly into a door casing. An outside corner will be a **miter joint.** Each inside corner will be cut as a **coped joint.** The **scarf joint** happens in the center of a wall (versus a corner) where the two pieces meet to give the look of continuity. You can do this at any angle you wish . . . most carpenters meet theirs at 45 degrees to avoid confusion. (If we're cutting several pieces before installing them we might do the scarf joint at 33 degrees so as not to get them mixed up with the mitered joints.) Last, there is a **mitered return.** You may not need this one: it's for modern homes where the room doesn't really have a door but a doorway. If you can't find where one room begins and the other ends on a wall, this joint will look nice.

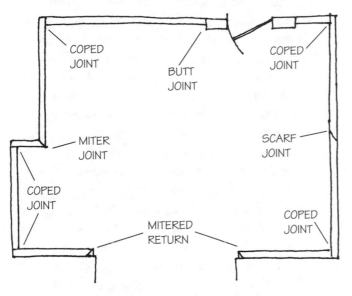

Locations of various joints in a room

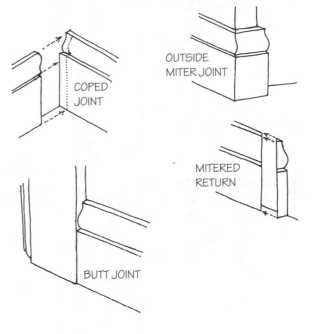

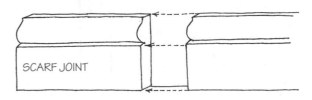

STEP 1 *To cut the first piece it's best to start with the long wall.* If you have a piece of molding that's longer than a long wall, great: you can do the whole wall in one piece. IF THERE IS CARPETING ON THE FLOOR THEN LIGHTLY PRESS THE MOLDING DOWN ALONG THE WALL BEFORE NAILING IN. Cut each end at 90 degrees to run directly into each side's perpendicular wall. To match two pieces in a scarf joint, try to cut the pieces so that (installed) they will sit on a stud. Nail your piece into the wall at the studs. At each stud drive one nail in toward the top of the base, on a raised portion of the profile (this will make it easier to fill later). Then drive the second nail in (at each stud) toward the bottom, and angle it down into the floor. Drive two nails on each end at an angle into its common stud.

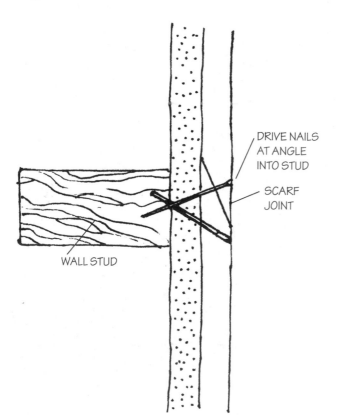

DRIVE NAILS AT ANGLE INTO STUD

SCARF JOINT

WALL STUD

STEP 2 *Cut the second piece.* Measure the distance between the door casing and the wall for this small piece. It will butt against the door casing and so needs a 90-degree cut on the left side. Cut the right side at a 45-degree angle and highlight the profile of the cut with your pencil . . . this will make it easier to follow with your coping saw to complete the coped joint. Cut along the profile to make a back bevel cut (at least at a 90-degree angle) just short of the

The Voice of Experience

MEASURE TWICE AND CUT ONCE I'm sure I had heard it before . . . I mean, it's been said often enough in the world of carpentry. Yet when my assistant, Ron, reminded me carefully of it once (he watched me screw something up and was trying to think of a polite way of broaching the subject) I realized that it was simple and would help me to avoid problems if I'd only *do it.* Several times I'd be at the installation stage of a just-constructed shelving unit and find that I measured all the shelves 1/4" too short . . . maybe I didn't take into account the amount of space I was losing from the routed sides. But I overconfidently had measured *only once* and so had to go back and re-cut the back panel and doors. Or we would cut a long length of base or crown molding that was supposed to end in an outside corner . . . and misread the tape by 1". Then we had to piece the wall length at the end. If we (*I*) had measured it twice chances are we would have caught the mistake. Ugh.

profile . . . maybe $1/16$". Finish taking off the remaining back bevel with your half-round and

three-square files until it sits squarely against your first piece with no gap.

Cut the second piece of the joint at a 45-degree angle.

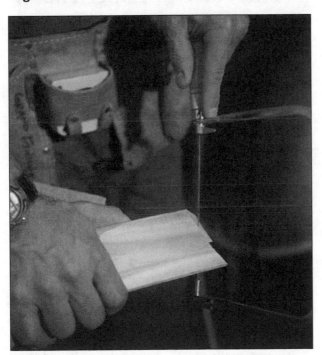

With the coping saw cut out the bevel back at least 90 degrees.

File the coped piece until it sits snugly against the butt joint piece.

STEP 3 *Cut the piece for the next wall.* Cut the left side of the piece at 45 degrees and cut out the back bevel for another nice coped joint. Leave the right side slightly longer than the corner, so that you can mark it once you've set the new piece in, with its coped left side joined temporarily. Mark it so that the front of the molding (the outside of the cut) will end about $1/8$" from the corner of the wall . . . any little amount short of the edge of the wall will give it a nice,

finished look. Now cut a piece and glue it to the end for a mitered return. You don't need to nail this piece and will probably split it if you do.

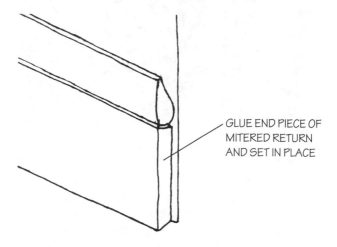

GLUE END PIECE OF MITERED RETURN AND SET IN PLACE

The Voice of Experience

YOU BE THE JUDGE If you screw up a little with the coping saw and take a little too much off when coping the profile, decide whether (1.) You have enough extra to recut the length and (2.) you feel like it. The mistake can probably be corrected with spackle or caulk when you do the finishing. When cutting a coped piece I've gotten into the habit of cutting that edge first and then following by making the cut at the other end of the piece of molding. This way if I screw up badly I can cut it off and try again and not lose too much to scrap. Once you get the hang of it, you can most probably skip the file step by cutting the back bevel off with your coping saw right along the profile. Cut carefully, and this will save a little time . . . you may still have to fine-tune the profile with the file but won't have to form the entire edge with it. On jobs that we really have to move I might set up a grinder with a $4\frac{1}{2}$" disc and, with goggles and mask, someone would grind the back bevel as someone else cuts, someone else installs, in assembly-line fashion.

The Voice of Experience

GREASE THE NAIL The wood may split upon nailing once in a while: it happens. To reduce chances of this happening, you can do a couple of things to the nail before you drive it into the molding. If you dip its tip in oil the lubrication will grease the new hole as the nail goes in. Sometimes I will spread a small pile of nails out on the drop cloth and lightly spray machine oil over it to get them all greased quickly. Ron (the carpenter who worked with me in California) would run each nail through his hair before he strikes it in place (he's got long hair and it's a little oily). You can also lightly blunt the tip of the nail and the dulled point will travel straight through the molding (versus the sharpened point catching the grain) and also lessen the chance of splitting.

I usually wait to complete one wall before I go back and set the nails. I wait just in case I run into a problem with the piece and it has to be lifted back off the wall. It certainly won't hurt if you do all the setting once the room is completely installed. With the nail set directly over the protruding head of the nail, a couple of taps are all it needs to push it just below the surface of the molding.

Set the nails into the surface of the wood with the nail set.

The Voice of Experience

Fit the base nicely to the floor: If your base configuration doesn't include a shoe you'll want to be sure that no obvious gaps show between the new base and the floor. Rarely will a floor be completely flat, and the older the floor the better the chances that it won't be. Before nailing each piece in, put it against the wall. Most small gaps will disappear if you nail one side in and then push the other side of the molding down with your foot as you nail the other side in. This will work 80% of the time if your base is under 4$\frac{1}{2}$". If it's larger, though, or if the floor has bulges that force the molding out of whack, there probably won't be any or enough give. Place the molding in place on the floor and then scribe the bottom of the cut piece, running your pencil flat against the floor along the area(s) that seem to present the problem. You should be able to shave these areas down with your block plane. Once you've got it down to where you're happy, follow up with a light sanding.

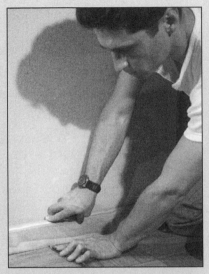

Run your carpenter's pencil flat along the floor to scribe (mark) where the floor gaps.

With the block plane, shave off the scribed areas until the base piece sits flush to the floor.

STEP 4 *Continue to measure, cut, and install the base molding around the room.* When you get to an outside corner, set the first piece a bit long on the wall and mark it by setting your try square or combination square against the surface of the wall it meets. Before nailing it in place mark the second piece the same way. Now check to see that the mitered ends close. If open either at the top or the bottom re-trim each piece by setting a piece of cardboard or thin end of a shim on the table of the saw. If the miter won't close, re-trim them slightly by setting the shim between the fence and the molding piece. The purpose is to remove a slight amount of the back bevel without cutting into the front outline of the profile. Often you can take the small amount down with either your block plane, utility knife, or even sandpaper and avoid shaving it with the saw. Use your 1¹⁄₄" brads to nail this corner together, as the 2" nails will probably split the wood.

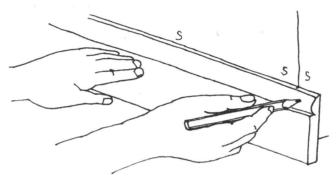

Hold the longer uncut piece to the corner and mark it for the miter cut.

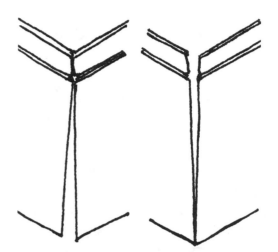

If outside miter doesn't close you can adjust the bevel with your block plane or re-shave with the chopsaw adjusting the angle with a piece of shim between the fence and the piece.

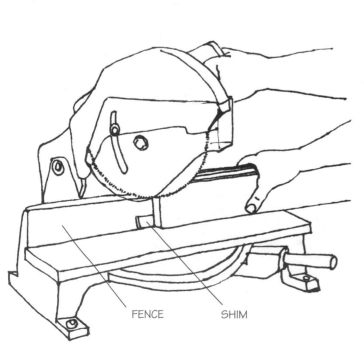

FENCE   SHIM

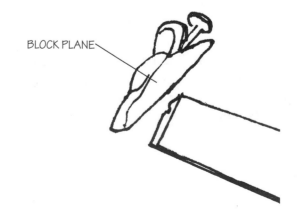

BLOCK PLANE

The Voice of Experience

WALL NOT FLAT? As you install your sections of base molding, you may encounter bulges and valleys in the walls. Many times the molding will contour somewhat to fit the wall. If you encounter a valley stick a shim piece in behind the base to fill the gap. Avoid pushing it in too far . . . just enough so that it keeps the molding piece running straight. Then hold the top of the shim and score the piece at the top of the base with your utility knife: careful not to let the knife slip and slice the top of the base. If there is a bulge in the wall there are several ways to handle it. You can take a little off the back of the molding with your block plane (adjusted for a low setting). Or you can gouge a small amount out of the wall, using the utility knife, bad chisel, and/or drywall grate. Each contractor will make his or her own choice, based on aesthetics, really. By shaving down the wall or the back of the molding, you may lose a portion of the profile at the top. If you shim the valleys on either side of the bulge, the base will not run perfectly in a straight line and may show up once finished. We tend to go with the former in order to preserve the line of the molding's profile and since the shimmed sections will be caulked anyway. If the bulges and valleys were very apparent then we might do a little of both.

With your utility knife slice the shim at the top of the base.

Remove the excess piece.

For gaps in the floor, pushing the base down with your heel as you nail it in place may do the trick.

Miterless Base

If the style suits you and it's the look you're going for, the lumber store may sell inside and outside corner blocks. These are prefabricated blocks that call for 90-degree butt joints at all corners. Besides the different "look" that it offers, it eliminates the call for inside coped and outside mitered joints. If you're using a hardwood this could make the job a lot easier to install.

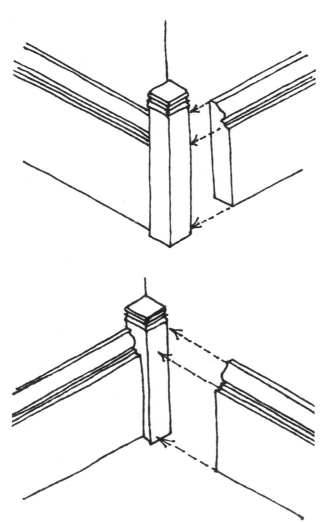

A miterless base is easy to install: the prefabricated inside and outside corner blocks require only butt joint cuts throughout.

The Voice of Experience

CURVED WALL? Set the circular saw to $1/8''$ and cut valleys in the back of the base piece. These grooves are called kerfs and should be spaced about $1/2''$ apart. When bent around a convex wall they close and allow the molding to contour to the wall. Conversely, the kerfs allow pliability for the piece to fit into a concave wall. Here they open up as the molding is bent to wall.

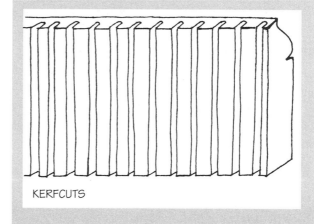

KERFCUTS

Cutting Angles Other Than 45 Degrees

MOST CORNERS, WHETHER INSIDE OR OUT, will be 45 degrees. Occasionally, though, you'll come to an unconventional corner. Your home could be very modern and the room could have more than four walls. Or it could be an old space with bay windows and have two inside and two outside corners to figure. Depending upon the depth of this alcove, for instance, your corners could be $22^1/_2$ degrees or somewhere around 33 degrees. Or the builder could have been completely unconventional and thrown in some obscure angle. FOR ODD INSIDE OR OUTSIDE CORNERS take your adjustable T-bevel and set it at the corner to gauge the angle. With the handle of the T-bevel sitting on one wall at the corner, the blade should extend out equally from between both walls. To determine this center point you can set an uncut piece on the floor and draw the outline on the floor. This will give you a fairly reliable dissecting point. You can now transfer this angle to the chop saw by lining the handle of the T-

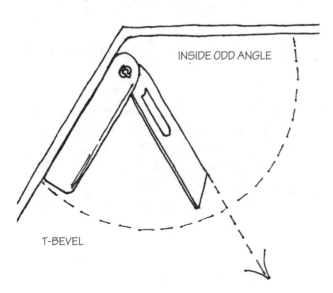

INSIDE ODD ANGLE

T-BEVEL

The Voice of Experience

If you are installing a multiple-piece base molding, the layout, cuts, and installation are pretty much the same as for a single-piece. It obviously takes more time to do a three- or two-piece base installation. However, the main board does not have to be coped or mitered for inside corners. Both sides can be cut at 90 degrees for a butt joint. Follow by coping the base cap for a nice fit and look.

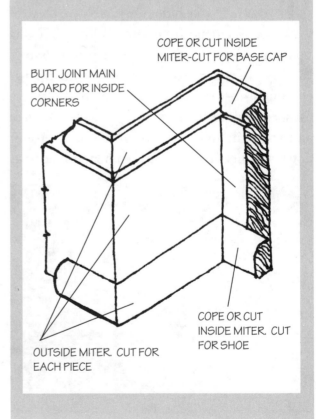

COPE OR CUT INSIDE
MITER-CUT FOR BASE CAP

BUTT JOINT MAIN
BOARD FOR INSIDE
CORNERS

OUTSIDE MITER. CUT FOR
EACH PIECE

COPE OR CUT
INSIDE MITER. CUT
FOR SHOE

bevel against the fence and then adjusting the blade of the saw to the new angle. Try out the angle with a couple of scraps first. When you know that you've got the angle down, then cut your actual piece. Accuracy is more important for the outside corner because the profile of each piece must meet up for the miter joint. So again, line up the T-bevel with the center/dissecting point, transfer it to the saw, and make several test cuts with scrap to be sure the pieces will close nicely on that outside miter (before you make the actual cuts).

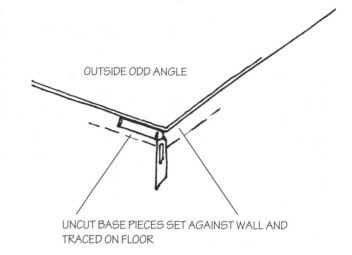

OUTSIDE ODD ANGLE

UNCUT BASE PIECES SET AGAINST WALL AND TRACED ON FLOOR

Finish with the Shoe Molding?

THIS COULD OR COULD NOT BE THE LOOK YOU want. It will hide any cracks or crevices between the new base molding and the floor, thus allowing you to skip the planing/saber-sawing-of-the-bottom-of-the-molding-to-contour-it-to-the-floor step. It could also give a finished look to the base. As you cut each piece and install it along the foot of the base, push it down so it fits snugly along the floor and the base.

Use 1¼" brads to tack it in place, and set the nails with the nail set. You can cope the corners like the base, but it's not really necessary: 45-degree cuts will close together just fine most of the time. When you get to spots where the base has butted into the door casing, you can either leave it with a bevel cut (more common) or fashion a mitered return (much nicer look).

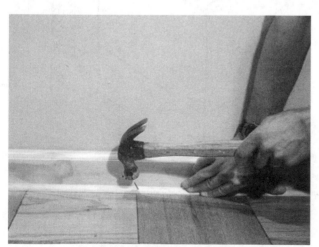

Push the shoe down as you go along and nail it in with 1 ¼" brads every foot or so.

The Voice of Experience

Hardwoods call for piloted holes: If you have gone with a hardwood like oak then figure on drilling a pilot hole for each nail before trying to drive it in. Choose a bit for your drill that is *slightly* smaller than the nail and you should be able to get the nail driven in, as well as avoid splitting the wood.

CHAPTER 2

Install a Wainscoting

History of the Wainscoting

WHAT IS A WAINSCOTING? THE WORD **wainscot** appeared in the English language in 1570 and it's defined in the dictionary as paneling that covers the lower portion of the wall (this portion is also called the dado). It is usually made of wood and encompasses the base molding. Technically a wainscoting is comprised of the base molding, the dado, and the dado cap (also called the wainscot cap or chair rail). You've seen it in the photos of elegant French châteaus as well as in the House of the Seven Gables (if you've gone on that tour) in old Salem, Massachusetts. It originated for the same reason as moldings did: to *finish* off the room, lend a little charm, and hide the irregularities where the floor meets the wall. It's also believed by some that the additional paneling on the walls helped the home retain much-needed heat during the winter months.

In olden days the main room would often be the *only* room and so would serve multiple purposes. During breakfast and lunch the dining table and chairs (or benches) would sit in the center of the room and accommodate the large family and possible farmhands or neighbors.

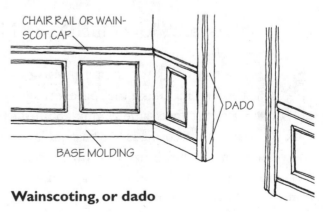

CHAIR RAIL OR WAIN-SCOT CAP

DADO

BASE MOLDING

Wainscoting, or dado

When not in use, the chairs and even the table were usually placed against the walls so as to leave the room free for occupying the sewing, washing, and other chores. At dinner the chairs and table were once again put in place and afterward lined back up against the wall for the night. If the family was exceptionally large, beds might even be brought out at this point to turn the main room into sleeping quarters. The wainscoting protected the walls from this constant re-configuring of the room.

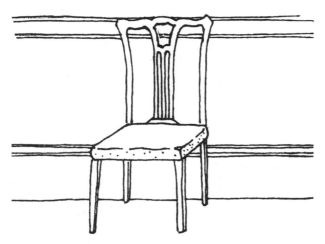

Even in larger, wealthier homes the wainscoting was still intended to protect the walls and wall coverings from the scuffing and marking of chairs and buffet tables. The height of the back of the chair usually corresponded to the center of the horizontally laid molding at the top of the lower wainscot. A fine home would have twelve or more chairs, available for dinner parties and guests. When not in use these extra chairs would be placed against the wall. The molding here is called the chair rail or cap. A typical height for the chair rail today is between 32" and 36".

There are several heights for a wainscoting. Puritans installed six-foot-high paneling with a top cap called a plate rail. This wide (usually about 6" or 7" deep) flat molding had a groove in it to allow plates for storage and display and to prevent them from falling. You might not see as many high wainscotings installed today, although don't let that stop you: it can add a richness to your room, filling it with paneled walls.

The word *wainscoting* usually refers to the entire package of paneling framed horizontally at the top by the chair rail molding and the bottom with a base molding. The wainscot paneling can be tongue-in-groove pieces fitted together vertically with bumps (sometimes called beading) and grooves. Or it can be simply strips of panel molding installed in squares. You might find the squares of panel molding in more formal rooms like dining rooms, living rooms, or entry hallways.

Assess How Much You'll Need and Purchase the Wood

MEASURE THE PERIMETER OF THE ROOM OR area, not including the space for doorways. Set that aside. Think about the look you want. Wainscoting is like base molding: you can design and customize your own style.

There are three basic wainscoting configurations, and I'll walk you through the installation of each. The materials (wood) needed will be based on the typical 36" height wainscoting, though if you've decided upon a higher or lower one, just adjust your calculations accordingly. Depending upon which of the following projects you choose to do, determine the amounts of each kind of wood you'll need. Once armed with

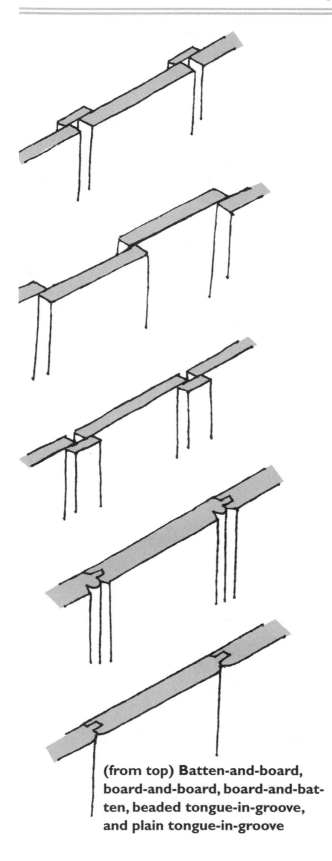

(from top) **Batten-and-board, board-and-board, board-and-batten, beaded tongue-in-groove, and plain tongue-in-groove**

the numbers, re-read "Assess How Much You'll Need and Purchase the Moldings" in chapter 1: "Install a Base Molding" for footage/stock purchase suggestions.

THE FIRST IS A **SOLID WOOD WAINSCOTING.** THESE are installed vertically on the wall. The batten and board, board and board, and board and batten date back to Colonial times and encompass the Shaker as well as the Mission styles. Most commonly found in lumber stores are the tongue-in-groove pieces, with smooth or beaded available in various widths. This is the first project laid out in the following pages. WOOD NEEDED: $1/2"$ x 2" wood strips (for furring out wall: can also use $1/2"$ x 3"), poplar or knotty pine will do (ask at the lumber store what inexpensive softwood they have in stock that would work in this capacity). You can go around and manually count every 16" or so how many 3' strips you'll need. Or take the perimeter of the room in feet (leave out doorways but include window areas), multiply by 12 (to get it in inches), divide by 16 (to get how often on the wall the strips will be installed), and multiply by 3. For both the wainscoting cap and the base molding, measure the perimeter of the room for footage needs.

SECOND, THERE IS THE MORE ELEGANT **SOLID WOOD-paneled wainscoting**, also called horizontal solid wood. It was found in more formal settings and can add a richness to the dining room or reading room. This style requires the installation of at least two layers of wood to duplicate the fullness and the depth of the style.

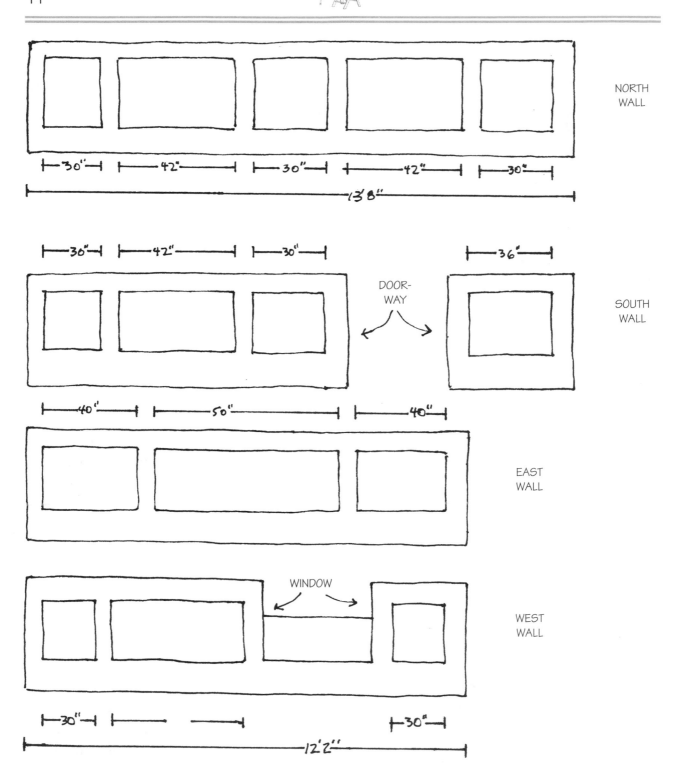

Measure your room and create your own wainscoting design, wall by wall.

Here I've chosen the simple, elegant look of recessed squares. The profiles chosen for defining the squares should be similar in look and style to the base and cap. The formula for this project will be ½" paneling with ¾" framing, with molding to trim it. Treating each wall separately, plan/draw the design with the intended panel size. WOOD NEEDED: Measure the perimeter of the room and divide by 8. This will tell you how many 4' x 8' sheets of MDF to buy. (If the finish wainscot will be finished with stain and/or polyurethane, then purchase ½" birch shop plywood for the paneling.) Take the perimeter of the room and multiply by 2 to determine the amount of 1" x 4" poplar to get. (The 1" x 4" will be used as the facing running horizontally along the top and vertically as the sides.) The perimeter of the room (including window spaces but not including doorways) will give you the amount needed for the 1" x 8" poplar (the 1" x 8" will be run as facing horizontally along the bottom, to balance out the base molding's height), each of the cap moldings (there are two profiles in this project's design), and the base molding. (NOTE: The base chosen here is 3½" high. If you decide on purchasing a higher base, then figure in a wider facing strip to run horizontally along the floor to balance out the base's height accordingly.) Last you will need the small molding to trim the insides of each new square created. There generally is a big waste factor with this piece. Multiply the perimeter of the room by 4 and add 10% to get the amount of ogee molding needed.

THE THIRD CONFIGURATION IS CALLED **PANEL MOLDing wainscoting.** It is not a *real* wood wainscoting but rather a configuration of molding installations that once set in place give the *illusion* of solid wood wainscot panels. The first wainscoting I ever created was like this. A client of mine in New York wanted the look of a paneled wainscoting but didn't want to go the expense of a full-scale solid wood installation because she lived in a rental apartment. The walls were relatively smooth. Once the panel molding and chair rail were set in place on the wall and caulked, I painted a uniform white semi-gloss finish from the base to the chair rail. It so gave the room an elegant feel of wood-paneled wainscoting that I went home and did the same in *my* own *rental* apartment. Draw a design with location/measurements for each wall. WOOD NEEDED: Multiple the perimeter of the room by 4 to get the amount of panel molding. (It wouldn't hurt to add another 10 to 20%, as this stuff is relatively inexpensive and there is a pretty big waste factor.) Then the perimeter of the room will give you the footage needed for the chair rail.

IF YOU'RE GOING AHEAD WITH ONE OF THE FIRST two projects, solid wood or solid wood-paneled wainscoting, now would be a good time to remove the old base molding (if there is any). Follow the steps from "Prepwork: Remove the Old Molding and Locate the Studs" in chapter 1.

MATERIALS CHECKLIST

Note: One or two of the following may not be needed,
depending upon which wainscoting project you opted for.

- [ ] Wood and molding
- [ ] Power chop saw
- [ ] Paint thinner; rag (for excess adhesive)
- [ ] Pneumatic nail gun and Compressor (if possible)
- [ ] Saber saw
- [ ] Circular saw
- [ ] Crosscut or backsaw
- [ ] Coping saw
- [ ] Flush-cut saw
- [ ] Level (24")
- [ ] Torpedo level
- [ ] Safety glasses
- [ ] Stud finder (battery-powered)
- [ ] Panel adhesive tubes; caulk gun (if installing panels)
- [ ] Adjustable T-bevel (if your room has any corners other than 45 degrees)
- [ ] End-cutter pliers
- [ ] Shims
- [ ] Half-round and three-square file

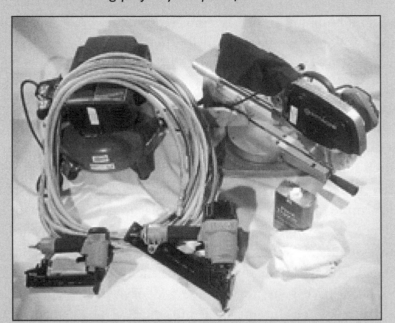

- ☐ Wood glue
- ☐ Nail set
- ☐ Pencil
- ☐ Utility knife
- ☐ Tape measure
- ☐ Blue painter's tape
- ☐ Claw or ripping hammer
- ☐ 2" 6D and 1½" 4D finish nails
- ☐ 1¼" 3D brads
- ☐ Block plane

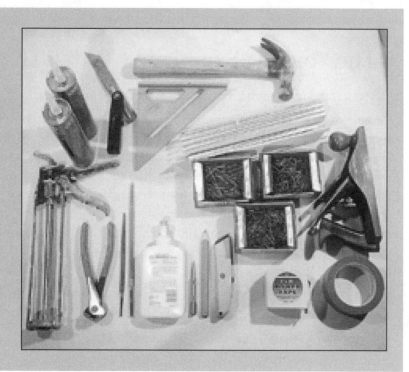

Solid Wood Wainscoting *(Tongue-in-Groove)*

STEP 1 *Mark the height of the new wainscoting.* Measure up 36" from the floor in one place and then go around the room and pencil the line where the *bottom* edge of the wainscot cap will sit. Use the level, and be as accurate as you can. The room may slope and so the distance from the floor at one point in the room (36") may be vastly different from the distance from the floor at another point (36¾"). This way, your wainscoting will still be level, which is the most important thing, for both looks as well as ease in keeping the project plumb during installation.

STEP 2 *Locate and mark the studs.* Move around the room with your electronic stud

Carry the horizontal line (where top of wainscot cap will sit) around the room. Locate studs and mark them the length of the dado with the 24-inch level.

The Voice of Experience

Remember: it's *not an exact science*. These electronic stud finders are the best tool for locating the hidden supports within the walls, but even the most seasoned professional has to play with them a bit while reading for accuracy. Even Ron, my co-worker and an experienced carpenter, *hated* trying to read the electronic stud finder, instead preferring to tap the wall and drive nails in blindly to determine the layout of the room's studs.

The Voice of Experience

As with the base installation, lay a handful of the 2" finish nails out on a cloth and lightly spray them with the oil or WD 40, tap-blunt the ends, *or* run the sharpened end through your hair just before striking it. Remember, this will help prevent the wood from splitting when you drive the nail in.

finder and mark the stud location. Double-check each one and lightly pencil the wall in two places: at the point just *above* where the finished wainscot cap will sit and down toward the floor, a couple of inches up. Draw vertical lines now at the locations using the level. All vertical studs within the wall won't be off-level more than a degree or so, and so the level will confirm whether the readings from the stud finder were accurate.

STEP 3 *Install furring strips.* Cut and install the $\frac{1}{2}$" x 2" (or $\frac{1}{2}$" x 4") wood at three places horizontally on the walls: line the top edge at the level line, the second strip at the floor, and the third at a center spot. Use the 2" finish nails, securing them at the studs (use pneumatic nail gun with compressor if you've got it), and use the level as you nail in the center strip.

Nail the $\frac{1}{2}$"x 2" furring strips horizontally around the room. Check the level of each strip as you nail it in.

STEP 4 *Start at the outside corner.* If there isn't one in the room begin at an inside corner. Cut each piece of tongue-in-groove paneling in the chop saw to size. I usually cut them ¼" to ½" shorter and line up the top with the top edge of the top furring strip. Set the circular saw to a 45-degree angle and rip two pieces to meet at a mitered joint. OR rip one edge to form a butt joint.

STEP 5 *Nail in the pieces.* Drive the 1½" finish nails in through the tongue, into the furring strips. Take care not to split the tongue, as it must be intact for the following piece's groove to be able to fit right over it.

The Voice of Experience

THIN FUR? Chances are that a wainscoting that was installed when the house was built was nailed directly into blocking installed and notched horizontally into the studding. To duplicate this now with your finished unwainscoted walls, you would have to cut out the drywall/plaster from the lower portion of the wall (a LOT of work, and messy, too). The furring strips in this project replace the blocking and offer a firm point of fastening for the paneling. And there are fire codes today in some states that actually demand there be a layer of drywall between the studding and the wainscot panels. Your new wainscoting will come out into the room a bit farther than wall, though, which is why I suggest using 1/2" thick strips, to limit that amount.

Set your circular saw or trim saw at a 45-degree angle to make the cut for an outside corner.

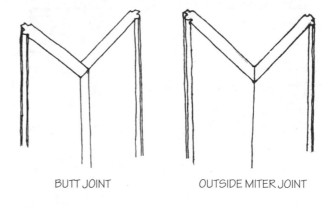

BUTT JOINT   OUTSIDE MITER JOINT

FURRING STRIP

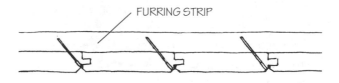

Nail each piece into the tongue at an angle, fastening it to the furring strip.

The Voice of Experience

TO *FUR* OR NOT TO *FUR? Glue* is the question. When I lived in San Francisco in a *rented* apartment I wanted to spruce up my water closet with a "wainscotty" feel but wasn't in the mood for too much work, since it was such a small room: maybe 12 square feet. The general thickness available for the tongue-in-groove paneling is ½". I found a variation of the typical beaded style at a home store known more for bargains than quality . . . it was only ³⁄₈" thick. So I decided to forgo the furring strips and use panel adhesive instead. It comes in tubes and can be applied with a caulking gun on the wall. The nails, though missing studs (and mostly just driving through the panels into the plaster wall), worked fine in combination with the adhesive, because the wood was pretty thin (and thus light) and the room itself was compact.

Apply the construction adhesive directly to the wall, keeping about 2 feet ahead of the installation direction.

STEP 6 *Cut and nail in the second piece.* Cut yourself a *hammering block* from a piece of scrap and use it to fit the second piece onto the corner piece. This will enable you to continue the installation without damaging the tongues *or* the grooves of any pieces and allow you to get each piece to fit nice and snug before moving on. Continue to check the "plumbness" every few pieces with your torpedo level before nailing.

Use a scrap piece as a hammering block to avoid damaging the tongue.

Periodically check the plumb of your installation with the torpedo level.

The Voice of Experience

TAP IT IN, BUT NOT *TOO* TIGHT Fit the groove onto the tongue of each successive piece, but avoid hammering them in too snugly. They should fit nice and close, but with a $^1/_{16}$" gap, to allow for expansion after the installation is complete. The wood will probably be sealed (with either stain or primer/paint) and the seasons will come and go: leaving a tiny gap will prevent possible future buckling of your wainscoting through all this. If you have something that is $^1/_{16}$" thick to use as a guide, great. I usually use a rigid piece of cardboard of that thickness: setting it in place before tapping in the adjoining strip.

STEP 7 *Continue cutting and installing the tongue-in-groove pieces around the room.* Keep checking every few pieces to be sure your installation hasn't gone out of plumb.

The Voice of Experience

WRAP THE CAP Chances are that the depth of your new wainscoting panels has come close to or has met the surface of the casings in the room. There are several ways to end the cap at those spots (window or door casing). You can notch it and wrap it over onto the casing (say, between $^3/_4$" and 1"). The end can be sanded or returned (with a return miter), or a return miter could be cut to end *at* the casing, to also give a nice, finished return.

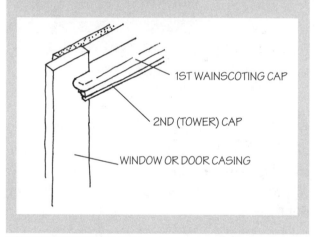

1ST WAINSCOTING CAP

2ND (TOWER) CAP

WINDOW OR DOOR CASING

STEP 8 *Cut and install the cap.* To install the first of the two-piece cap, measure each length as you go using the chop saw, and miter both the inside and outside corners. If more than one piece is needed to complete a wall, you can use any angle for the *scarf joint:* I usually use 22$^1/_2$ degrees for one. Use the 2" finish nails and drive them into the wall at an angle, fastening them to the studs. Set in 1$^1/_2$" nails at a steeper angle to fasten the cap to the furring strips. Set them with the nail set.

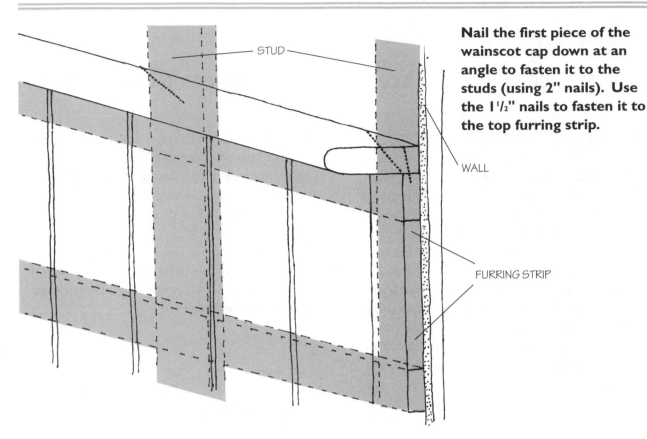

Nail the first piece of the wainscot cap down at an angle to fasten it to the studs (using 2" nails). Use the 1½" nails to fasten it to the top furring strip.

STUD

WALL

FURRING STRIP

STEP 9 *Install the base molding.* Follow the direction in chapter 1 to install the base. You can skip over the *location of the studs* part, as you now have solid wood on the wall all along the floor now.

The Voice of Experience

When you come to an inside corner and a full piece won't fit in the space left, measure that distance at both the top and the bottom. Use the saber saw to trim the piece to fit and a block plane to shave the last bit down. Now you can tap it in place with a scrap piece.

The Voice of Experience

For corners other than 45 degrees use your adjustable T-bevel to gauge the angle. By aligning the T-bevel to the blade of the chop saw, move the table of the saw until you've matched the angle (at least by eye). As with the base, test a few pieces of scrap before cutting the actual piece, and you should be fine. For precision angle match, see "Cutting Angles Other Than 45 Degrees" in chapter 1.

The Voice of Experience

DEALING WITH SWITCHES AND OUTLET RECEPTACLES

MATERIALS CHECKLIST

- [ ] $^3/_8$" drill
- [ ] $^5/_{16}$" drill bit, $^3/_4$" or $^1/_2$" bore bit
- [ ] Saber saw and blade for cutting wood
- [ ] Electrical tape
- [ ] 4-in-1 screwdriver
- [ ] Plastic junction box (NOTE: some locales only sell and allow metal to be used/installed; check local codes)
- [ ] Wire cutters
- [ ] Chisel
- [ ] Outlet receptacle or switch replacement
- [ ] Pencil
- [ ] Hammer

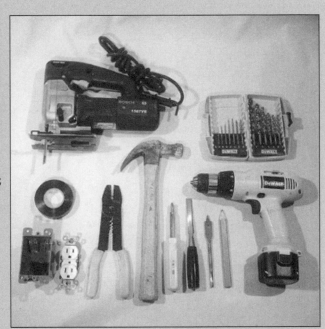

I'm not particularly fond of working with electricity, and the older the home the more confusing and complicated the wiring can be. That said, it's also a reality that with many home improvement projects you're going to come across electricity and have to deal with it, because it's almost impossible to hire a professional electrician to come and work on something as simple as relocating a switch or outlet receptacle to the outside of a wainscoting or base panel from its position on the wall. And it really *is* pretty straightforward.

(Continued)

1. CUT THE POWER. Protect yourself by shutting off the current to this particular place by finding the panel box or fuse box. Whether the switches or fuses are labeled or not, turn each one off one at a time, checking whether you've located the correct switch/fuse by either calling out to a partner or returning to the area yourself after each test.

2. REMOVE THE OUTLET OR SWITCH FROM THE WALL. Unscrew it at the top and bottom and carefully pull it out, *wires still attached,* as far as you can to determine how much play you've got with the wire. Although you've cut the power, avoid touching the sides unnecessarily: instead handle the outlet or switch by the top and bottom brackets.

3. CUT THE HOLE IN YOUR WAINSCOT PANEL OR BASE PIECE. Determine the location by measuring where the new wood will sit once in place. Trace the outline of your new plastic box onto the back of the wood panel where it will sit. Using the bore bit, drill several holes in the corners to make it easier to maneuver the saber saw around the outline. Finish cutting out the new hole with the saber saw.

4. UNHOOK THE WIRES FROM THE OLD RECEPTACLE. If they are older and not color-coded (black and white) or if there are several attached to specific screws on the old outlet then label them as you unhook them, for easy transfer to the new receptacle.

5. FIT THE NEW BOX IN PLACE. In the hole you've just cut: Screw it in place. The screws will tighten catches on the back of the panel and hold it there.

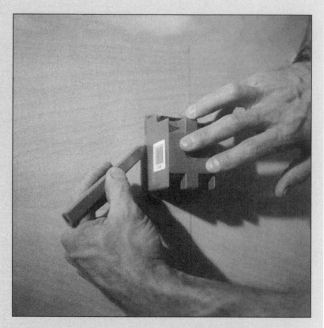

Trace the outline of your new junction box on the *back* of the panel where it will sit in the wall.

Drill holes with the ¹/₂" bore bit in the corners of the outline and cut out the shape with the saber saw.

Turn the panel around, fit the box, and screw in place. Pull the wire through the back of the box.

6. WIDEN THE HOLE IN THE WALL. If the original location in the wall needs widening for the back of the box to be able to sit once the panel is in place, then do it now. You may have to remove any old box and open the hole in the wall, using the chisel and hammer.

7. GUIDE THE WIRE THROUGH THE BACK OF THE BOX. Whether it is metal or plastic there will be several locations that you can tap an opening through the box, using a hammer and chisel or nail set. Install the panel in place with the wires pulled through.

8. HOOK UP THE NEW RECEPTACLE. Now turn the power back on and test it to be sure you re-wired it correctly.

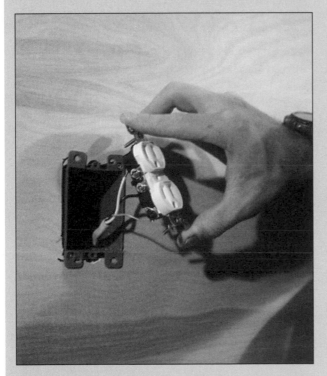

Affix the new panel to the wall and hook up the new receptacle.

Screw the receptacle into the box.

Solid Wood-Paneled Wainscoting

STEP 1 *Mark the height of the wainscoting.* Once you've decide on how high you want the new panels to come, measure up from the floor at one point and then mark the horizontal line around the room with the level and pencil. Professionals will usually use a chalk line for this; however, marking with the level and pencil will enable you to perform this step alone (you need two people to snap a chalk line).

STEP 2 *Locate and mark the studs.* Pencil an "S" on the wall just above your chosen horizontal line or mark it with a piece of blue painter's tape. Put a piece of tape on the floor at the corresponding stud location.

STEP 3 *Cut and install the ¹/₂" stock on the walls.* Apply panel adhesive to the backs of the panels using the caulking gun. Nail them at the studs with the 2" finish nails. Don't worry if there is a bit of a gap at the bottom: be sure to line the plywood to your horizontal level line.

Use blue painter's tape on the floor and wall to note the location of the studs.

The Voice of Experience

MEETING A WINDOW   If the wainscoting ends up being deeper than the window casing and apron, then you may want to re-install these portions to have the new piece wrap the facing of the panel. See chapter 4: "Install a Door or Window Casing" for details.

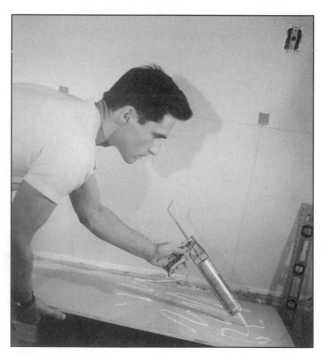

Apply panel adhesive to the back of the ¹/₂-inch panels before nailing to the wall.

STEP 4 *Cut and nail the lower and upper horizontal stock to the panels.* The longer the pieces, the better. Use the chop saw to cut the strips and apply wood glue or panel adhesive to the backs. Fasten them at the studs with 2" finish nails. Try to plan the seams for the corners of the squares. Double-check the lower strip with either the torpedo level or the 24" level before nailing it in.

STEP 5 *Cut and install the vertical strips to form the squares.* Again, apply an adhesive, either the wood glue or panel adhesive, to the backs of the pieces. Continue to check that they are plumb with the torpedo level. Nail them into the ½" stock. To ensure that the vertical strips are flush with the horizontal strips, drive the 1½" finish nails in where necessary, following with the nail set. If there's any excess adhesive squishing out and visible, wipe it thoroughly off now, using the rag with a little bit of paint thinner. The glue can be cleaned off with a little warm water on the rag.

STEP 6 *Cut and install the ogee molding on the inside of each square.* Use the chop saw to miter each corner at 45 degrees. Wood glue should hold it in nicely: follow with two or three 1½" finish nails for each piece.

STEP 7 *Cut and install the cap.* As before, the longer the strips the better. Use the chop saw and make miter cuts for the inside and the outside corners. Cut and install the cap. To install the first of the two-piece cap, measure each length as you go using the chop saw, and miter both the inside and outside corners. If more than one piece is needed to complete a wall, you can use any angle for the scarf joint: I usu-

Check the lower strips for level before nailing them in.

Check the vertical strips for plumb as you nail them in.

Cut the ogee molding at 45 degrees and fit inside the squares: wood glue and 1 ¹/₂-inch nails should do the trick.

Drive the 2-inch nails through the cap at an angle at each stud location.

ally use 22¹/₂ degrees for one. Use the 2" finish nails and drive them into the wall at an angle every foot or so. Set in 1¹/₂" nails every few feet or so at a steeper angle to fasten the cap to the panels. Repeat this with the second profile using the 1¹/₂" nails. Set them with the nail set.

STEP 8 *Cut and install the base.* Follow the steps for installing base molding in chapter 1, skipping the *stud-location* step.

Panel Molding Wainscoting

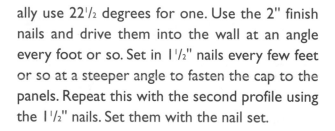

THIS IS THE SIMPLEST OF THE INSTALLATIONS and can be incorporated into the room with the existing base molding. This one mimics somewhat the look of the solid wood panels installed previously.

STEP 1 *Draw the wainscoting configuration on the wall.* First bring the 24" level around the room to pencil in where the top of the chair rail molding will sit (36"). Then draw your squares, again using the level: for both the vertical and horizontal lines that will make up the box.

STEP 2 *Locate and mark the studs.* Use the stud finder and put a small piece of blue tape just above the horizontal chair rail line.

STEP 3 *Cut and install the chair rail.* Using the chop saw to cut the pieces, miter the outside

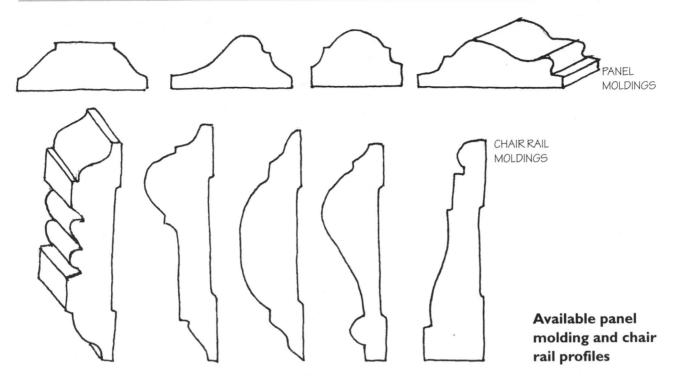

PANEL MOLDINGS

CHAIR RAIL MOLDINGS

Available panel molding and chair rail profiles

corners, and cope the inside ones (with the coping saw). As in base molding and wainscoting cap installations, cut any necessary scarf joints at $22^1/_2$ or $33^1/_3$ degrees, nailing the overlapping piece accordingly.

STEP 4 *Cut and install the panel molding.* Use the chop saw to cut each corner at 45 degrees. Double-check that the opposing pair pieces of each square are equal in length to ensure that the corners will close snugly. Apply some panel

Using a tape measure and the 24-inch level, draw your wainscoting configuration on the wall.

Install the chair rail molding.

Cut and install the panel molding squares.

adhesive to the back of each piece and then secure them in place with the $1^3/_4$" finish nails. The walls may not be perfectly flat, and you won't be nailing at the studs, so the squares may take a bit of fidgeting as you set each nail in with the nail set. Slide a shim in behind a corner, if necessary.

The Voice of Experience

Pre-fab squares can be pretty and ornate. Many molding stores offer variations of pre-fabricated panel molding to produce beautiful squares. This look is popular in San Francisco, where Victorian is the dominant style. It is often used on the wall *above* the wainscoting, in conjunction with the crown and/or picture molding, or even just as vast wall panels between the base molding and crown and/or picture molding. The installation is the same as earlier: adhesive with small finish nails to hold it in place (until the glue dries).

Panel molding squares above the chair rail

Panel molding squares with prefabricated corners

CHAPTER 3

Install a Crown Molding and/or Picture Molding

CEILINGS FROM THE EARLIEST DWELLINGS OF the civilized world consisted of wood. Just as the base molding was (and still is) used to hide the meeting of the walls at the floor, the crown originated to hide the juncture where the wall met the ceiling. First as a mask and then as a decoration, the crown really was the first official moulding that appeared with frequency. It can be seen in outstanding glory in drawings from the Greco-Roman era. By the 12th century crown mouldings were fashioned ornately from stone to complement Gothic churches as well as palaces and summer estates. (And by the twentieth century we here in America dropped the *u* and now just call it MOLDING.)

Choose a Style and Size

The crown molding sits in the corner where the ceiling meets the wall. The flat surfaces behind the board are positioned squarely on the ceiling as well as the wall surface. There are different ways that find it in position, where the distances from the corner to the end of the molding vary from the top to the bottom.

There are so many styles available today. The most common is considered the "coronado" crown. This profile or variations of it can be seen in illustrations of homes such as palaces dating back hundreds of years. It has two points, one at the top and one at the bottom. The center outward curve softens the edges and visually suggests that there is no cold inside corner behind it. It's available in sizes as small as $1^1/_2$" up to 10", though a size of $2^3/_4$"–$3^1/_2$" is found mostly in a room with 8'–9' walls. Conversely, a

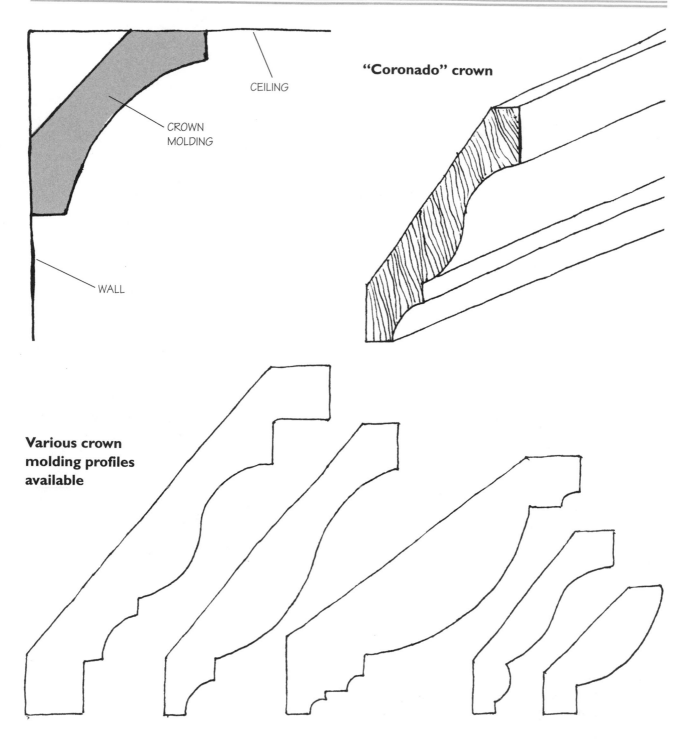

CEILING

CROWN
MOLDING

WALL

"Coronado" crown

**Various crown
molding profiles
available**

simple cove molding is also used, with the end
points to frame an inward curve, again disguis-
ing and softening the inside corner where the
ceiling meets the wall. Higher ceilings and ambi-
tion may suggest a multiple crown. Here the
style can be created by you as completely original simply by reorganizing crowns, coves, casings, and/or blocks.

Assess How Much You'll Need and Purchase the Molding

A S WITH ALL MOLDING INSTALLATIONS, COMmon sense tells you that it's wise to purchase a bit *more* than your total measurements. The angles that will be cut on the profile for each corner will become waste, and the bigger the molding, the bigger the waste factor. If you're going with a 2³/₄" molding, then getting 5–7% additional stock should qualify for a

MATERIALS CHECKLIST

- Molding stock
- Chop saw (and extension cord, if necessary)
- Tape measure
- Pencil
- Utility knife
- Claw hammer
- Nail set
- Shims
- 1¹/₄" 3D brads and 2¹/₂" 8D finish nails
- Chalk line
- Wood glue
- T-bevel
- Pneumatic nail gun (optional)
- Drill, bits (if working with a hardwood)
- Safety glasses
- Stepladder
- Coping saw
- Three-square file
- Round file

(Not pictured here: coping saw, 3-square file, and round file.)

complete job without the need of a second run to the lumber store (while the job is in progress). The larger the molding profile, though, usually will translate to more waste while installing, and so call for more stock on hand. I never really had it translated scientifically but would guestimate: a $3^1/_2$" piece would usually cause me to purchase at least 10% more than the room's measurements. In other words, if the room's footage total was 100', I would purchase 110'. A larger molding of $4^1/_2$" and I would get 115'–120' (15–20% more).

Figure what the vertical projection would be for your molding. In other words, where your crown will sit installed on the wall. Double-check with a scrap piece and mark it in several places along the wall, especially in the corners, to have a point of reference. This is a good time to note how un-*straight* the ceiling might be: if there are significant high or low spots. Pull a chalk line along the wall (a partner would be helpful at this point) with the guidance of your marks from either corner. You'll be hard pressed to find a perfect ceiling. The top of the crown will sit flush against the ceiling on low points with the high points shimmed at the nail site and later caulked.

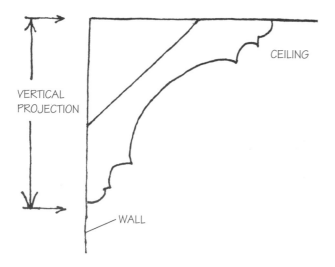

STEP 1 *Locate and mark the studs and lay out the room.* Go around the room and note the location of the studs with the blue tape. By avoiding too much pencil on the wall, you can limit the amount of finishing (priming/painting) at the end of the job. Though not *completely* necessary, the more information you know about the location of the joists in the ceiling (like which way they run, for example) the better. Unless you're working with a drywalled room, the joists aren't always easy to locate. If you can determine which walls they intersect perpendicularly, mark the spots (also with blue tape).

Locate the studs and mark them just below the vertical projection on the wall with blue tape.

And whether cutting in a miter box or on a chop saw, the carpenter's rule of thumb is back-ward-and-upside-down against the fence. The exception is larger profiles that are too big to stand on the table, against the fence, and under the blade. For those molding profiles (usually over $4^1/_2$", which is the largest that will stand up under the blade of a basic 12" chop saw), a slide compound saw is needed. The blade slices forward and back on a pipe and is also hinged to move to the side. These two features enable you to get an accurate 45-degree cut on a much larger profile. My 8¹/₂" slide compound saw can handle a crown up to 8¹/₄", for instance. I can never remember the settings since we install so few of the really big crowns, so I just double-check the instruction manual. It's got the positioning of the turntable as

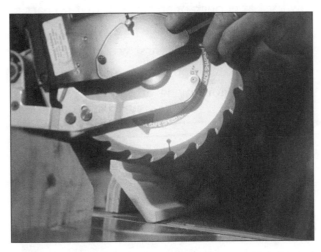

Crown molding is placed upside down and backward against the fence of the saw for accurate cuts.

The Voice of Experience

JUST THE TWO OF US I've put in many crown installations with*out* the aid of an assistant, but the job will go much smoother with two pairs of hands. From the chalk mark to the measuring and holding up of the long pieces for nailing, a second person can ensure an accurate installation.

The Voice of Experience

To Glue or Not to Glue, that is the question. I've seen professionals do it both ways, each swearing that theirs was *the best* way to do it. For most jobs, especially in newer homes or apartment buildings, I will not apply an adhesive to the back of the crown. However I will consider this if (1.) in older construction; (2.) I'm not confident as to the location of the ceiling joists or the depth of the plaster/lathe surfaces; (3.) the ceiling surfaces are crumbly or not incredibly sound and re-surfacing them is not an option; or (4.) I'm installing a really big crown. This way I'll be assured that a month after the job is complete the client won't have to call me and tell me that the caulk line has separated at the top and/or bottom where the crown was installed. After each piece is cut and once it's checked for accuracy at its new position, apply a bead of latex panel adhesive using a caulking gun to the top back surface and the bottom back surface. Once the piece is nailed in place, wipe off any excess glue with a wet sponge, rag, or damp paper towel.

Apply panel adhesive to the back of each cut strip before nailing it in place.

well as the tilt of the head (bevel angle) listed for each required cut, whether it be an inside or outside corner.

STEP 2 *Cut and install the crown.* The first piece should butt the wall at 90 degrees on each side.

Start wherever you'd like: I usually began on the long wall and used a scarf joint, enabling me to install the wall with two pieces. 2½" finish nails work nicely to fasten most sizes of crown to the studding. (If working with a hardwood, like oak, you'll want to pilot the holes before nailing to avoid splitting the molding. For this you would use a bit that is slightly smaller than

the nail size and a drill.) Making the long wall take the butt joints is generally easier for me to install, because the perpendicular walls that need to be coped are shorter.

As we move around the room, the next piece needs to be coped on the end that will meet/rest at the end of the first wall to form the first inside corner. As with the base molding installation, cut your end (upside down and at an angle) at 45 degrees. Cut along the profile with your coping saw back at enough of an angle so that no part of the wood in back will interfere with the profile sitting snugly against the first wall's end piece. It's not difficult to slip and destroy part of your profile if you're not paying attention. So if you're

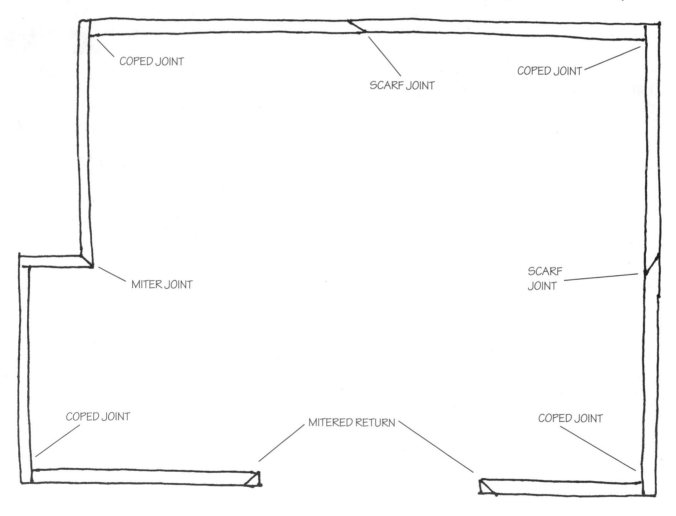

COPED JOINT

SCARF JOINT

COPED JOINT

MITER JOINT

SCARF JOINT

COPED JOINT

MITERED RETURN

COPED JOINT

uncomfortable trying to make the cut with the coping saw *directly* along the profile's line, then guide your saw *within* the line about ¹/₁₆". Then finish it off with your files: a round file and/or a three-square file, depending upon what this crown's particular profile calls for. Many professionals work their coped joints this way.

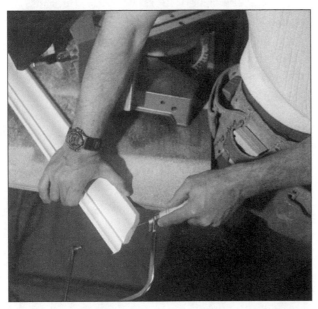

After you cut the strip at a 45-degree angle, cut the back bevel out with the coping saw.

Fine-tune the coped cut with files until it sits snugly against the butt joint (already installed).

The Voice of Experience

As with a base molding installation, there are five joints: the **butt joint, coped joint, scarf joint, miter joint,** and **mitered return.** The concept is *basically* the same. A 90-degree cut for when the crown dies into a wall and doesn't continue is a butt joint. The outside corner is two pieces mitered to meet, extending from that corner (miter joint). The inside corner comprised of one piece butted to the wall and a perpendicular piece coped to fit onto it is a coped joint. When the wall extends out into another room, a mitered return may be called for. These first four are cut with the molding sitting upside-down-and-backward against the fence. And you can make your scarf joint the same. However, since you want these two pieces to meet and appear as one, although you want at least some angle between them, the less you have, the better. Adjust the miter angle to 33¹/₃ and lay the molding flat on the table. The meeting of the two pieces will be brief and you'll have a better chance of nailing it seamless together at a stud.

STEP 3 *Set the nails.* I generally wait till I've installed the second wall before I set the nails on the first wall. It really serves no purpose except to give me security . . . in case some tweaking needs doing . . . I might come across an unseen bow in the ceiling that will necessitate some shimming behind the crown on the first piece, either at the wall or the ceiling, for instance.

The Voice of Experience

Nail through the crown at a place that will drive directly through the back and into the wall stud (or ceiling joist). The spot on the profile should also be an easy one to fill the nail holes (as in when you finish the molding). A good place to nail through on a coronado-style crown, for instance, would be either a flat or larger concave or convex as follows. A difficult place to fill would be a small concave spot.

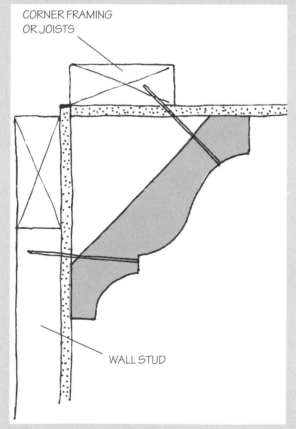

CORNER FRAMING OR JOISTS

WALL STUD

Location of nails into "coronado" crown profile.

The Voice of Experience

SHIM? A small recess here and there is common and a shim will ensure that the crown sits flat at every nailed spot. As with the nails, I usually wait until I'm on the second wall before I go back and complete the previous wall/ceiling. In this case, by cutting the excess off each shim. Angle your utility knife in just slightly so the cut piece is *just* beyond the edge of the crown. This way, when you finish up later with caulk you'll be confident that the shim won't show. It's a minor point, but the caulk is supposed to "fool" the eye into seeing the crown sitting flush all along the installation, and a shim that shows up as a small bump only distracts the eye from seeing the line as continuous.

Shim the crown where it doesn't sit flush, either at the wall or ceiling. Slice off excess with utility knife.

Mitering an Outside Corner

WHEN YOU GET TO AN OUTSIDE CORNER, chances are the angle will require a 45-degree cut. However, you could be going around and into a set of bay windows. Whether you have to determine the miter angle or not, it will probably take a little adjusting. So it's always good if the other end of your piece that has the outside angle is *butted* at the wall, enabling you a *little* bit of leeway in filing or shaving the profile to get it to meet the other profile snugly. A bulge in the wall may be pushing your pieces apart, preventing them from meeting. As with the base molding, if you can't *bend* the crown (*just a bit*) to enable it to meet the other piece, you can shave out a portion of the wall.

Once you get the joint to close nicely, spread some wood glue on the inside of each edge and set the ends together with 1¹⁄₄" brads.

Use the smaller brads to set the outside corners together.

The Voice of Experience

Most of the time an outside corner fits just fine. One of the problems that happens occasionally is that the miter may have a gap . . . the pieces don't close. You can shave off a bit of the back by adjusting the chop saw by a degree. Usually I'll place a small wedge scrap between the fence and the piece to re-cut it (just like with the base) and shave the back a bit . . . leaving the gauge intact. Or you can usually shave the excess off from the back with a file.

The Voice of Experience

Not only is there a miterless base available but also a MITERLESS CROWN. Check with the local lumberyard if you're interested. It's comprised of inside and outside corner blocks, thus eliminating the need for any miter cutting . . . all the lengths are butt joints. This may be a good choice if you want to simplify the installation, especially if you're working with a hardwood and it's your first job. Because you don't have to worry about any of the *adjustments* you may have made to the inside and outside corners (that end up getting caulked or puttied), finishing with stain and/or polyurethane is a viable option, even for the beginner.

Figuring the Angles Other Than 45 Degrees

A S WITH THE BASE MOLDING, MOST CORNERS, whether inside or out, will be 45 degrees. However, to determine the angle for odd inside and outside corners see chapter 1. "Install a Base Molding" ("Cutting the Angles Other Than 45 Degrees"). Instead of tracing the molding on the *floor,* scribe where it will sit on the *ceiling.*

Multiple-Piece Crown

I F YOU'VE GOT A HIGH CEILING AND ARE ADVEN- turous and fairly ambitious, creating your own crown by combining several profiles into an installation can be rewarding. A casing can be combined with a stock crown to elongate it . . . whether simple or ornate it can be beautiful.

First cut and construct a sample version of your configuration so you can get the distances for both the vertical and horizontal projections.

Transfer the measurements to both the ceiling and the walls. If part of your stock will sit flush on the ceiling, make your cuts by sitting the molding flat on the chop saw turntable. If there will be a profile sitting flush on the wall, then make your miter cuts by placing the molding flat against the fence. These would be installed first, then the stock that sits on top, with new markings now transferred to the flat pieces as a guide.

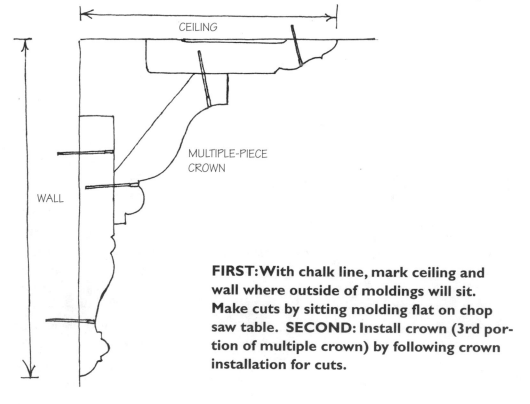

CEILING

MULTIPLE-PIECE
CROWN

WALL

FIRST: With chalk line, mark ceiling and wall where outside of moldings will sit. Make cuts by sitting molding flat on chop saw table. SECOND: Install crown (3rd portion of multiple crown) by following crown installation for cuts.

Picture Molding

ONE OF THE EARLY SIGNS THAT MAN HAD begun to stand apart from other animals was his recording of art on the walls of caves. For centuries (and still today, somewhat) drawings and paintings were done directly on walls. As civilization progressed, so did the complexity of his art as well as the way it was displayed.

By the Renaissance period beautiful paintings with ornate frames were being produced. Separate from the wall now, they could be moved to wherever was desired. To aid in the versatility of display came the picture molding. Running horizontally along the top of the wall, but not quite at the ceiling, it was *(and is)* an additional piece of ornament in the room.

But its main function was and is to support artwork. Paintings were hung by a thin rope (and later wire), either by two points going vertically up to the molding or meeting at a center point. The lower down the wire was attached on the back of the painting, the farther out the top would lean in its hanging position. Originally art was hung very high and so the angle of the painting thus would allow easy viewing from the ground. The art can be moved up or down or to the left or right without damage to the wall. Because of this ability to change both the actual display as well as just the location, many muse-

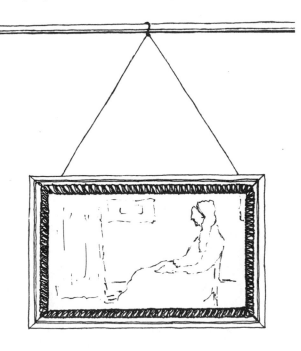

The Voice of Experience

My last apartment in San Francisco had coved 9' ceilings and a picture molding in each of the rooms: even in the stairwell and entryway. We attached small eyehooks on the backs of our pictures and suspended them with clear fishing wire, so it was almost invisible. This worked out really well. We were able to avoid damaging the walls by not making holes each time a location was chosen/changed. One of our framed prints was *really* heavy (almost 60 pounds), and we were able to hang it nicely with strong-enough fishing line. Because the building was the old lathe-and-plaster type, I'm sure I would have destroyed the walls putting a strong-enough hook up, even if a stud was located near to the spot decided upon. My favorite benefit was that once the pictures were hung level, they rarely moved. In the past I've always had to go around straightening wall artwork (because a crooked piece really bugs me).

ums hang their art in this fashion. (Look up the wall next time you drop into the Mellon Museum in Washington, D.C.)

Aesthetically, picture molding adds trim to the room. It breaks up the long expanse of the wall as it travels to the ceiling and can be used instead of or even in conjunction with a crown molding. A pleasing color scheme is usually to finish-paint any wall space left *above* the molding the same color/finish as the ceiling. This connects the room nicely and makes the ceiling look larger and higher, actually.

I've seen it installed almost *to* the ceiling, leaving only $\frac{1}{2}$" between the top of the molding and the ceiling. This was incorporated in homes with not-so-tall walls (8' to $8\frac{1}{2}$') in the 1930s and '40s. Over time, and lots of layers of paint and settlement, the molding would end up coming close and/or touching the ceiling so that somewhere along the line a painter would just *caulk* the remaining crevice. I've come across this often, where it almost looks like a little crown molding. A typical installation in a room with 9'

walls would be horizontally about 10+" down from the ceiling.

There are several molding profiles out there. A typical one is between $1\frac{3}{4}$" and $2\frac{1}{2}$", although there are larger and more ornate ones available. It's designed to work with picture rail hooks, which come in most forms of metal (brass, brass-plated, and nickel, for example).

Picture molding is the *easiest* to install. Measure the perimeter of the room at the approximate location of your installation to determine how much linear footage you'll need. As with all other moldings, get the longest pieces you can so you'll have the least amount of cuts. A good length to work with would be 12' or 14', depending upon how you transport it to the site of installation as well as how much room you have to work with/cut the molding there. As I mentioned with the base molding, the lumberyards get their stock in 16' pieces, so that length is available (though pretty difficult to transport or work with). Anything smaller than that (to about 6') can usually be had.

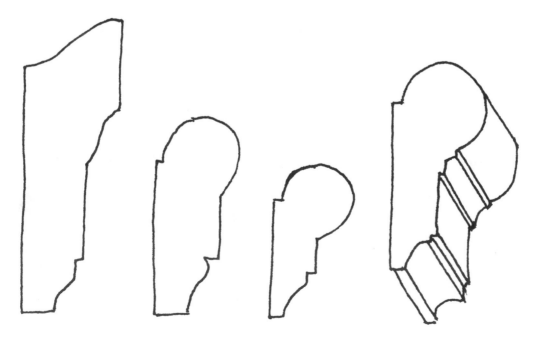

**Picture molding
profiles available**

MATERIALS CHECKLIST

- Molding stock
- Plastic miter box and 12" box saw OR chop saw (and extension cord, if necessary)
- Tape measure
- Pencil
- Utility knife
- Safety goggles
- Claw hammer
- Nail set
- 2" 6D finish nails
- 1¹/₄" 3D brads
- T-bevel, compass
- Stepladder
- Stud finder (battery-operated)
- Blue painter's tape
- Shims
- 24" level

STEP 1 *Decide on the desired location and mark it.* If you have a coved ceiling then the highest you'd want to put the molding is just at the point where the cove turns into flat wall. For a 9' ceiling the standard is around 10" from the ceiling. Use the level and draw a pencil line at the location, starting at one point in the room and continuing around from that one point of origin. Since the floor may not be entirely level itself, you'll give yourself a more accurate line if you avoid measuring/marking each wall separately.

STEP 2 *Locate and mark the studs.* Leave a small piece of the blue tape just below the mark.

STEP 3 *Cut and install the molding.* Coping the inside joints is entirely necessary for a small molding like this (1³/₄"–2¹/₂"). Measure each wall and cut the ends that will go into the corner at 45 degrees. If the piece isn't long enough, connect two with a scarf joint at a stud using 22½ or 33 degrees. If the pieces don't close absolutely perfect at the inside corners slide the thin part of a shim behind one or each piece at that corner, as needed.

Nail in the molding twice at each stud with the 2" finish nails at spots that will be quick and relatively painless to fill. Since the molding is small there will be a better chance of splitting the wood, so it won't hurt to "grease" the nail. Spray machine oil or some other lubricant on the nail before you hit it in: this will lessen the likelihood of splitting by greasing a path through the wood. Blunting the tip lightly with your hammer will do the same thing.

STEP 4 *Set the nails.* Join any outside corners with the brads and if there is a wall that doesn't

The Voice of Experience

If you have an odd-degree corner, you can determine it with your T-bevel at the floor. You can probably find the angle just as accurately if you test a few pieces of scraps at various degrees. This is a small molding and the exact measurement you find at the floor might not translate up the wall (exactly), but that shouldn't be a problem.

end in the room you're working in, finish it with a mitered return. Cut any shim excess by sliding the utility knife *just* inside the back of the molding.

CHAPTER 4

Install a Door
or Window Casing

A Little History of the Casing

THE FOCUS IN A ROOM DURING ANCIENT Greece and Rome was always the wall . . . so doors were really just openings to pass through. Windows were even less noticeable, being only slits in the wall so as not to take away from the walls. Neither had any ornamentation or framing at all. It really wasn't until the Gothic period when windows got larger and profiles (moldings) were added around them and around doors. By the 10th and 11th centuries there were actually windows (versus just openings) and in Europe moldings began to appear as decoration around windows and doors.

Replacement

THE INSTALLATION OF DOOR OR WINDOW CAS-ing is very straightforward, and so rather than lay it out in steps, let me go through the terms and some tips that will familiarize you with the process. Since the door casing goes to the floor, it should be done *before* any new base molding installation.

A door casing usually consists of two vertical pieces and a header. A nice variation to this is the addition of the plinth block, which sits at the floor, and the vertical casing dies into it with a butt joint. 3/4" wood (or "one-by") can be used, so long as the casing isn't deeper than the block. If the casing exceeds 3/4", then something in 7/8"

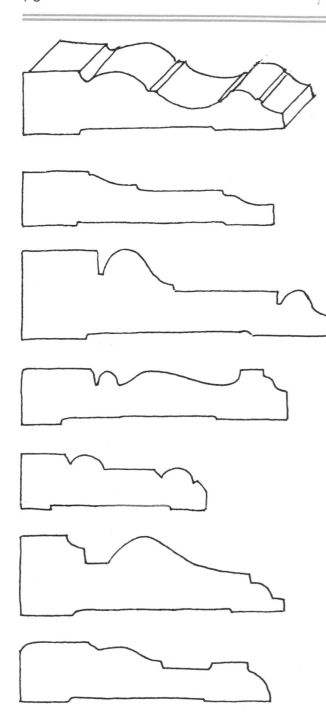

Casing profiles available

Casing is cut by placing the molding flat on the saw table.

or 1¼″ will give it substance and look more appropriate.

The top horizontal piece of the window casing is also called the header. The two sides meet the header with either a mitered cut or a butt joint. The mitered cut for a casing installation is called a flat miter because the molding is placed flat when cut. (When stood against the fence and cut, as for crown, base, and chair rail, the cut is called a vertical miter.) The header can be created with header blocks and/or a different or plain profile for the header. A simple yet beautiful variation can combine a thicker ⁷/₈″ wood for the header trimmed with a tiny crown profile and framed with a base profile.

Again, this applies to both the window and the door casing. Once you've chosen a style/configuration, remaining consistent between doors and windows within a room (or even the house) will add to the beauty and architecture. If choosing a base molding (or other installations, like crown and/or picture molding profiles), then again, try to stay within the same "family" of shapes.

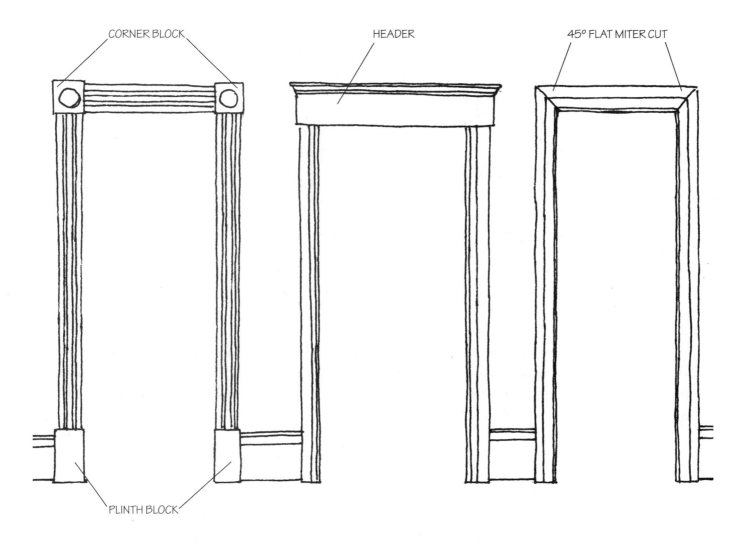

CORNER BLOCK

HEADER

45° FLAT MITER CUT

PLINTH BLOCK

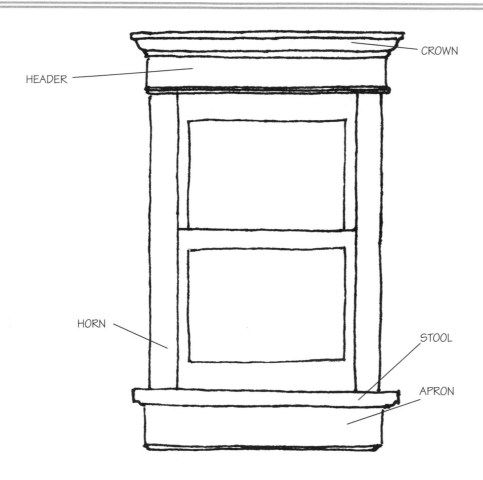

CROWN

HEADER

HORN

STOOL

APRON

The same molding profile can be used as the "bottom" casing for a window opening so that the window looks like a picture frame. However, most of the time there is a stool held up by an apron.

A WORD ABOUT PURCHASING THE CASING. AS I mentioned earlier in the book, moldings are milled and sent to the stores in 16' and 14' lengths. The lumber store wants to limit the amount of waste (unsellable leftover), so they will readily sell lengths cut from that size to 6' pieces. It is rare that they will want to cut you a

3' length of anything (unless it's an expensive hardwood, like oak threshold, for instance). When you are working on casing for an average-sized door frame (32" x 80") it makes sense then to purchase one 10' and one 7' length. The 7' can be used for one side and the 10' can be cut down for the header and the other side. If you are working on multiple door frames it is smart to assess not just the total footage needed but also how many 7' lengths will be needed as well as how many 3' lengths will be needed. The two main reasons for this careful planning is (1.) to avoid too much waste/scrap for yourself and (2.) to avoid having to make any scarf cuts for the casing installation.

MATERIALS CHECKLIST

- Molding stock
- Plastic miter box and 12" box saw OR chop saw (and extension cord, if necessary)
- Tape measure
- Pencil
- Utility knife
- Block plane
- Drywall grate plane
- 24" level
- Stepladder
- Stud finder (battery-operated)
- Blue painter's tape
- Torpedo level
- Shims

- 2" 6D finish nails
- 1¼" 4D brads
- Nail set
- Saber saw
- Safety goggles
- Claw hammer
- Combination square

Check the alignment of the wall to the door-jamb or window frame. Often the wall may need a bit of adjustment before installing the new casing. If the wall is "proud" (protrudes out), scribe the edge of the casing-to-be with the utility knife. Remove the casing, and "take down" the drywall/plaster wall using a combination of multiple utility knife cuts and running over the area with the drywall grate. If the jamb or frame itself is proud, simply shave it down with the block plane until it's flush.

Decide on a reveal. A typical one is between ⅛" and ¼". Mark it. Cut and install the vertical pieces first for the door using 2" finish nails every 16" to 24". Don't set any of the nails just yet. Before installing the header, wipe some wood glue on the inside grain of the cut. If the back corner doesn't close, stick a shim behind the corner, cutting it off later with the utility knife.

Double-check that the header is level by placing the torpedo level on top of it. Nail the header in every 8" to 10" into the jamb and three times at the top, with the center nail going through the stud. Finish by tapping one or two 1¹/₄" brads into the sides of the miter to hold the two pieces snugly and setting all the nails.

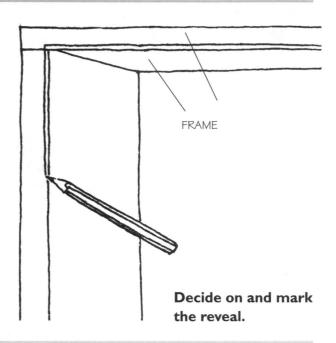

FRAME

Decide on and mark the reveal.

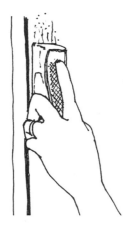

If the wall protrudes out farther than the frame, use your utility knife and drywall grate to shave until flush.

The Voice of Experience

CLOSING THE GAP When the window or door is not perfectly square you've got to still make the casing look like it is. If square, the toe and heel will close nicely. When the heel doesn't close or the toe doesn't close you may have to play around a bit to get a good cut. It may only take a little shaving in the back along the miter cut with the utility knife. You may be able to re-cut the piece by placing a shim or piece of cardboard between the fence of the chop saw and the molding. Or it could be just as easy as shaving a bit off with the block plane.

If the heel and toe don't close nicely, the end-grain of the header can be sanded, planed, or re-shaved on the chop saw.

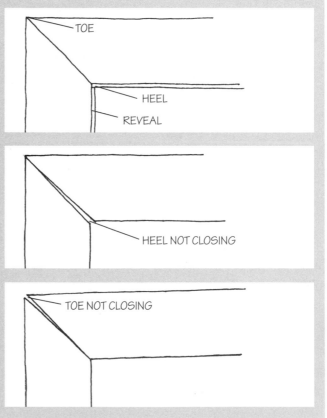

TOE

HEEL

REVEAL

HEEL NOT CLOSING

TOE NOT CLOSING

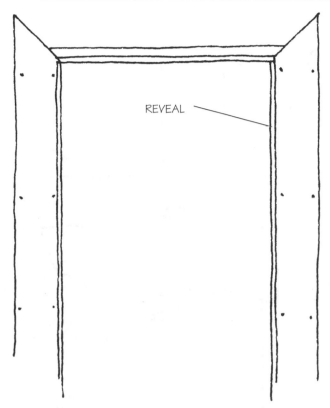

REVEAL

Install the vertical pieces.

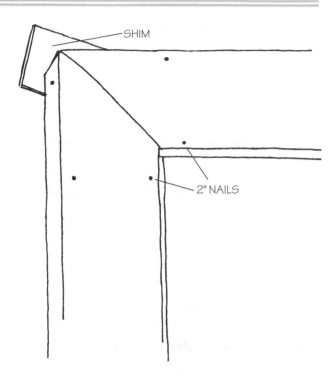

SHIM

2" NAILS

Install the header last and set all nails. Shim the back corner if that part of the wall is shallow. Apply wood glue to the end-grain before installing the header.

The Voice of Experience

CROOKED HOUSE Sometimes old houses settle and all plumbness and levelness is lost. If the doorway has really gone out of whack and you install the header completely level, it may look even worse. At times like these I try to find a middle point . . . usually by aligning the header halfway between level and the slope of the old doorway. The casing is really only trim (aesthetic). This way the eye is less likely to pick it up.

THE WINDOW CASING CAN BE A BIT MORE involved, taking the stool and apron into consideration. After marking the reveal, measure and mark where the casing will end at the stool. Typical stool profiles usually correspond to the particular window and sill. The length of the stool is determined by the width of the casing on either side and their reveals, plus the extended distance that the header is to be. This is usual, but not law. If the header is to be mitered I find that a $3/4''$ addition on either side does nicely.

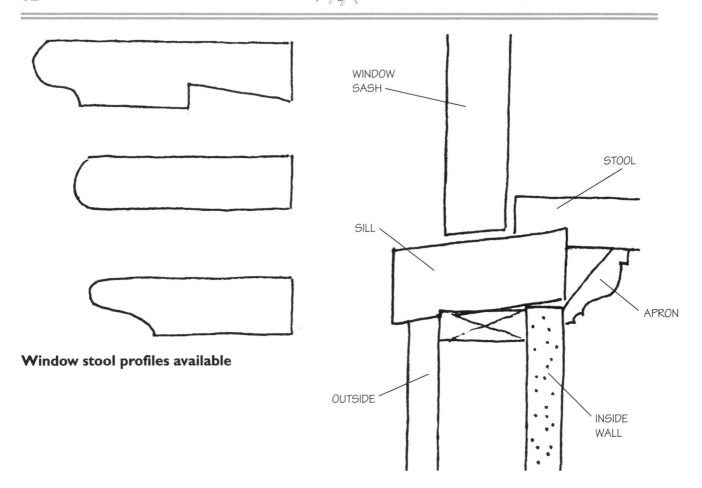

Window stool profiles available

STEP 1 *Mark the center line on the existing sill.*
Cut the stool to the finished length. Mark a center line on it with the combination square.

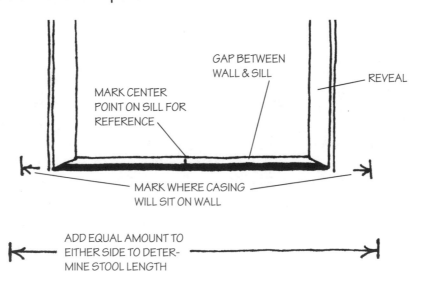

STEP 2 *Hold the stool in place against the wall, lining up the center marks.* Using your combination square, measure and mark the amount of stool that sits on the face of the wall on both the left and the right side. This is called the horn.

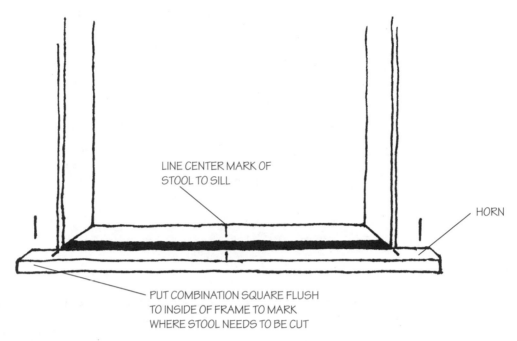

LINE CENTER MARK OF
STOOL TO SILL

HORN

PUT COMBINATION SQUARE FLUSH
TO INSIDE OF FRAME TO MARK
WHERE STOOL NEEDS TO BE CUT

STEP 3 *If the sill does not come flush to the inside wall surface, then notch these areas with your saber saw.* Before nailing in, shave/sand the edges to match the front somewhat. Line up the center line marks and drive several 2" finish nails down into frame at an angle.

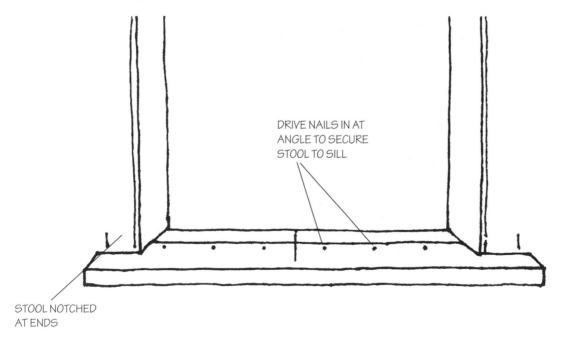

DRIVE NAILS IN AT
ANGLE TO SECURE
STOOL TO SILL

STOOL NOTCHED
AT ENDS

STEP 4 *The apron then can be cut (sized to the header) with two mitered returns,* one ready to be glued on either end. To help you hold it centered and in place and enable you to nail it properly, cut a length of scrap slightly longer than the distance between the floor and the apron and wedge it under the apron until it bows a bit. Now nail the apron in place, at either end and into the stud.

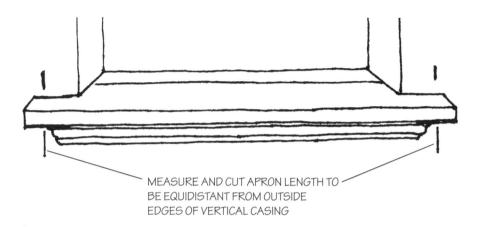

MEASURE AND CUT APRON LENGTH TO
BE EQUIDISTANT FROM OUTSIDE
EDGES OF VERTICAL CASING

STEP 5 *Follow with the side pieces of casing, driving in nails in pairs every 16" to 24".* Next, the header with an 8"–10" spacing for nails at the reveal and three nails at the top with the center one going into the stud. If the header is constructed with blocking and crown, put the header in first. Then cut and nail the long strips onto the header, completing the crown by gluing the side pieces on. Nail it in with a 1¼" brad, careful to avoid splitting the piece. Finish by gluing in the apron's mitered returns.

CHAPTER 5

Finishing

AH, FINISHING. THERE ARE ONLY TWO THINGS LEFT to do now before painting or staining/ polyure-thaning the new woodwork: fill the nail holes and caulk the cracks. So . . .

Fill the Nail Holes and Caulk the Cracks

WORKING WITH THE TWO PUTTY KNIVES, fill in the nail holes with the lightweight spackle (or latex wood fill). I like lightweight spackle because it shrinks very little and rather than a full second round of filling usually only requires a light touching up. Push the spackle in with one knife and drag the excess off the surface of the molding with the other knife. The less left on the wood the less that will have to be sanded after. If the project is to be finished with stain and polyurethane, then use the latex wood filler instead of the spackle.

The spackle dries pretty quickly and I usually check it a couple of hours after the first filler coat. Some holes may need a second touch-up fill, so get them now. Another few hours and you can sand the holes lightly with the 100-grit sandpaper or the flexible sanding block. The flexible blocks work nicely, especially around the contours of a crown or chair rail's profile. If the finish is going to be stain/polyurethane, then you'll have to go around and lightly sand the entire face of the profile. The molding and wood will more than likely have a light "film" on it, formed since coming out of the mill and being handled and from sitting in the lumber store. If the wood isn't sanded now to make the surface equally receptive to the new sealer it will more likely than not look blotchy and all-around unprofessional (something you certainly don't want after all your WORK!).

The Voice of Experience

FILL 'ER UP If your moldings are to be finished with stain and/or polyurethane, you should be able to find a good-quality latex-based wood filler in an assortment of wood product matches. However, there may be a large crevice, hole, or ding that needs repair and you aren't real happy with the closest match available in the product you found for your wood. If you mix some sanded scrapings from your project into the filler before application, the dried patch should then be as close to invisible as you'll find.

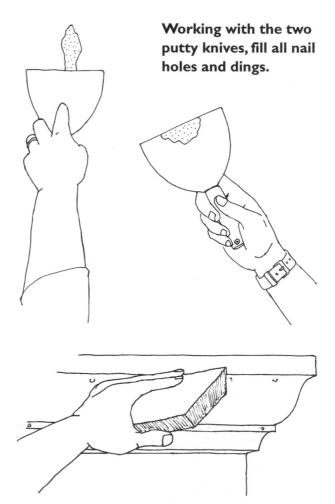

Working with the two putty knives, fill all nail holes and dings.

Sand the filled holes in the crown and other contoured profiles with the flexible sponge sander.

And if you're planning on finishing with a stain/polyurethane, then hold off on the caulking: it should be done AFTER the wood is sealed.

Cut the nose of the caulk tube at an angle and load it into the gun. Run a bead of caulk into the outside crevices of the crown, wainscoting, picture molding, and door/window casings. If the project is going to be finished with primer/paint, then caulk *all* crevices, even within the wainscoting or a multiple crown. Wipe out the excess first with the wet sponge and then with your wet finger, continually rinsing the sponge and wiping your finger clean on the rag.

Most paintable caulks can be painted over once a skin forms, sometimes as early as an hour after caulking. Though the primer or paint will slow the process somewhat, the caulk will continue to cure nevertheless.

The Voice of Experience

Crevice between the new base molding and the floor? Chances are that you've gotten your new base to fit close enough to the floor, or that a shoe was included to close any gap between the base molding and the floor. But maybe not. We came on to a job to do the finishing work on a newly constructed home in the Potrero Hill district of San Francisco. There were slight gaps at the floor here and there. I didn't think it was that noticeable, but the builder/owner was an incredibly meticulous man (though not that careful of a carpenter: I mean, otherwise he wouldn't have left the gaps) and insisted that we "fill" it. It was so slight that I thought that (1.) wood filler would probably pop out of the crack and (2.) we probably couldn't even get wood filler *in* to the tiny crevice, anyway. So we ran blue tape along the floor just under the base (where there was a gap) and just up on the base (where it touched the floor). Then I went around the rooms and caulked at the crevices between the blue tape (on the floor) and the base. After priming and painting and another few days for drying/curing, I went around with a fresh razor blade and made a clean cut between the tape and the finished base. At this point I was able to carefully tear up the tape and *voilà!* Seamless new base!

The Voice of Experience

DON'T RUSH Read the directions of the caulk. All caulk products are different, and some *cannot* be painted over for 24–48 hours afterward. When I visited my mom at the new house she and her husband had contracted to have built, the first thing I noticed was the hairline crack where the baseboard had separated from the wall. The house was only a year old. I began to look around and noticed that virtually everywhere the caulk had been applied (above the base molding throughout and even where the casings met the wall) there was a tiny separation. The molding seemed to be installed soundly, yet the failure of the caulking to seal the crevices was evident because most probably the finishing of the house had been rushed. Once the caulk is dry be sure to prime over it.

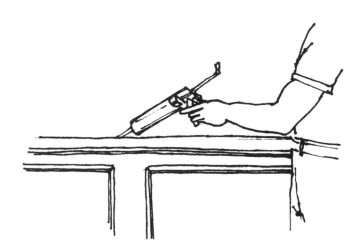

**Caulk any gaps in your new molding configu-
rations: where they touch the wall, ceiling,
and each other.**

Prime and Paint the Molding

MATERIALS CHECKLIST

- ☐ Paint
- ☐ Primer
- ☐ Paint can opener
- ☐ Single-edge razor blades (10) (optional)
- ☐ 4" putty knife
- ☐ Spray shellac, can
- ☐ 2½" sash brush
- ☐ Metal "toothbrush" brush cleaner
- ☐ Blue painter's tape
- ☐ Cotton rag
- ☐ Drop cloth or newspaper

IF PART OF THE CARPENTRY PROJECT WAS BASE molding, then lay blue tape along the wood floor at the molding JUST UP ON THE MOLDING, about ¹/₁₆". This will seal the molding and prevent primer and paint from bleeding down to the floor. If you merely put the tape *at* the floor, the paint *will* bleed through in places: it's inevitable. I've even let the tape ride up ¹/₈" onto the new base in places. Yet once it is removed, all you see is a very clear straight line. Because the floor is wood also, it's very difficult for the human eye to pick up that fraction of an inch of unpainted base way down there by the floor. But a little amount of paint bled onto the floor is very easy to see and breaks up the continuity that a freshly painted line gives your beautiful new carpentry installation.

If the base molding was installed in a carpeted room, then place the blue tape strips on the carpet at the base with enough extra to go down into the crevice (which will protect the carpeting from any paint getting around the tape). Push it in with the putty knife.

Prime the new wood. Even if the wood was pre-primed, you want to at least go around and prime over the filled/sanded nail holes, as they

Lay the blue painter's tape along the base, going just up on the molding ¹/₁₆ inches. Push it in with a putty knife.

will show up after the finish paint is applied. The reason I brush the entire wainscoting is because a roller will leave the surface with a "stippled" effect, which I think looks kind of cheesy. If you weren't planning on re-painting the walls that the new molding touches, hopefully you have some extra paint for touch-up, because you're priming now over the wood as well as the caulking at the wall. After the primer paint is dry, if a knot still bleeds through, spray it with the shellac primer.

I approach each project a little differently for the finish painting, because of two reasons:

1. *Flat paints (what the walls and ceilings probably are) are much easier to "cut in" than satin/semi-gloss finish (what the new molding probably is) paints.*

2. *Paint lines at lower levels read differently to the human eye than lines at high points.*

The Voice of Experience

A KNOT IS A KNOT IS A KNOT When I was seven I remember watching my dad on a Saturday morning carefully brushing shellac over the stumps of three small birch trees that he'd just cut down. We lived in a very wooded new development and he was trying to clear away some of the yard. He explained to me that the shellac would prevent the pitch from oozing out of the tree and getting on us kids when we were playing in the yard. Everyone who at one time or another has inadvertently touched a pine tree and gotten pitch on his or her hands knows how sticky and difficult to clean off it is. Home shop guys and gals will have mineral spirits on hand to clean off any oozing through from wood knots that gets on their hands. That is *generally* not a problem with the moldings that come from the mill and are sold in the lumber store. They have been kiln-dried, which will usually dry out any residue of pitch left in the wood. However, and especially with pine, you may come across some. By keeping a can of clear spray shellac handy, you can stop any bleeding through that is discovered after the primer and before the finish painting.

Let me illustrate.

Base Molding

Prime it first, going up a little onto the wall (maybe an inch or so). Once it is dry, then do the walls, whether re-painting or just touching

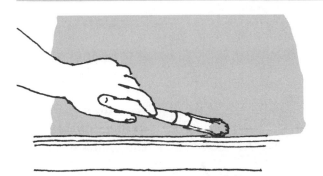

For the finish painting, first paint/touch-up the wall, going slightly onto base molding.

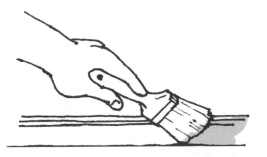

Then paint the base. Cut in your line just up onto the wall $\frac{1}{16}$-inch to $\frac{1}{8}$-inch. You'll be able to get a cleaner line and the eye will accept the base as finished.

up at the base, and go down onto the base just a bit. Now for a little trick if you are using a latex (water-based) paint. For the finish painting have a putty knife and empty box or small trash can with you. As you paint the base now allow your brush and the paint to go up onto the wall maybe $\frac{1}{8}$". This will enable you to get a much straighter line than if you attempted to cut in with the brush at the precise line where the base meets the wall. And the eye will see this as "clean." The blue tape will most probably pull off the setting *(and even dry)* new paint if you wait to pull it up. So as you go along and paint the base, remove the portion of tape, every 4'–6' or so, that is at the freshly painted section. This way the paint will not have a chance to set up at all.

The alternative is to slice the tape with a razor blade and remove it once the paint is dry. We've done it this way, but it's far more time-consuming than just removing it as you go along. If you've been using an alkyd (oil-based) paint then wait a day or two for everything to dry and remove the tape all at once: it won't pull the new paint off the molding.

Wainscoting

Follow the same steps as with the base molding. The new line you've created up onto the line (just above the wainscot cap) will read cleaner to the human eye than if you tried to stay *at* the line where the cap meets the wall.

Crown

Prime the new crown, and be sure to cover the new caulking at the top and bottom. Go onto the ceiling and the wall. Next re-paint or touch-up the ceiling, going onto the crown molding just a bit. Then paint the crown, cutting in at the top just below the point where the crown touches the ceiling. Paint down onto the wall a bit; maybe $\frac{3}{4}$"–1". Finish with cutting in the wall

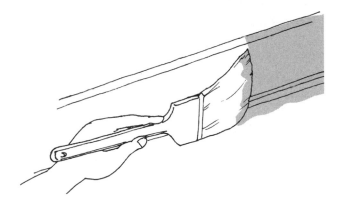

Cut in crown molding paint at ceiling and go onto wall a bit.

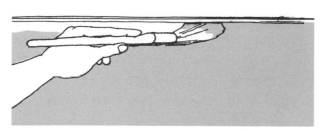

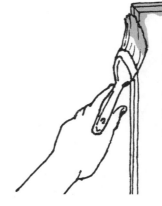

Once the crown is dry, paint/touch-up the walls by cutting in at the caulk line.

If the panel molding is to be a different color from the wall, then paint it first, going onto the wall a bit.

paint just at the caulked place where the crown meets the wall. If you go up onto the crown a bit, that's okay: it's difficult to see and will look clean and fresh.

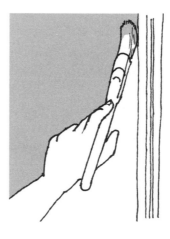

Then paint/touch-up the walls by cutting in with the wall color at the edge of the molding on both sides.

Picture or Panel Molding

Prime and paint the entire molding first, going over onto the wall a bit. Once it is dry, finish with the wall color to cut in at the molding.

Or Stain and/or Polyurethane the Molding

MATERIALS CHECKLIST

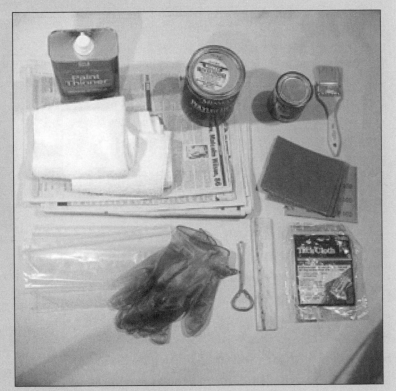

- Stain
- Several clean, absorbent rags
- Paint can opener
- Latex gloves
- Mixing stick
- Tack cloth
- Sandpaper, 100 grit, or sanding block
- Polyurethane
- 2" pure bristle brush(es)
- "Zipper" freezer bag
- Mineral spirits
- Drop cloth or newspaper

STAINING IS MESSY; SO IS POLYURETHANING. SO if you're going this way it's best to leave any ceiling or wall painting until *after*. Lightly sand the new wood with the sanding block or 100-grit sandpaper. Pay particular attention around the filled spots to be sure you've sanded any excess filler, as well as blended the surrounding area to these sanded spots. Follow by wiping the wood with the tack cloth to clean off the fine wood-dust particles. Use the zipper freezer bag to dispose of the used stain rags. **The linseed oil in stains could cause rags left in open air to spontaneously combust.**

Run the sandpaper or sanding block over the wood, carefully sanding excess filler off surface around the holes.

The Voice of Experience

ONE-STEP? There are many products available now that combine the stain and polyurethane in one coat. They are not bad; however, once you've applied the finish you cannot wipe off any excess, a step that I think enables you to give the wood a clean, finished look. Nor can you put on a second coat of stain with the expectation of modifying the result by trying to get the wood a bit darker or richer.

Apply the stain with a brush, working a panel or so at a time.

If the wood is getting only polyurethane (and not stain) then skip over this step. Put on a pair of latex gloves and mix the stain thoroughly before applying. Put it on with a brush and follow by wiping the excess off with a clean rag. Follow the directions on the particular stain product you bought as to drying times. Generally it will be ready within six or so hours to receive either another stain coat or the polyurethane.

Again, sand the wood, this time only *lightly* wiping the surface with the block or paper. Wipe clean with the tack cloth. Like stain, polyurethane's components separate easily, so be sure to stir/mix it well before applying. Apply with the pure bristle brush but realize that polyurethane will sag and run much more freely than paint, so don't be too liberal.

Once the polyurethane is dry (sitting at least overnight) you can now caulk the crevices where the new molding meets the wall. Because the wood is sealed now it will be easy to wipe the excess caulk off the wood. If this was done *before*

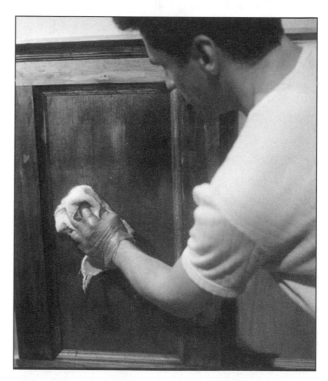

Wipe off excess with a rag, then continue to stain, repeating the steps.

Whether staining or just applying urethane, lightly sand and wipe clean with a tack cloth between each step.

the wood was sealed the caulk would have seeped into the wood at the edges and caused the stain/polyurethane to seal the wood unevenly.

Now follow once more with a light sand: this will remove any little bubbles or dust particles that got trapped in the last coat. Wipe clean, and apply the polyurethane coat. The crown, panel molding, or base should look great now. A wainscoting, like a wood floor, will look better with a third coat, however; you be the judge. Once the polyurethane is dry the finish paint can be done on the ceiling and/or walls: you're out of danger of any new paint getting absorbed into new wood. If you do make a mistake and get paint onto the wood now it can be easily wiped off.

Earth-Friendly and Odor-Free

A WATER-BASED CLEAR COATING WITHOUT epoxy resins is called urethane. It doesn't smell, is easy to work with, and doesn't give your wood that amber color (the yellow is actually a component of the polyurethane resin): the wood is dried completely naturally. Since it is water-based, there's no need for mineral spirits or the pure bristle brush: use a regular paintbrush and clean up afterward with warm water and soap. I've always thought that this is a much nicer look than the epoxy-resin (oil-based) finish. And during the drying process it doesn't release VOCs (Volatile Organic Compounds) like its amber-colored cousin, which are murder on the human respiratory tract. A nicer look . . . so easy on the eyes, good for your lungs, and better for the environment.

GLOSSARY

apron: the horizontal portion of molding that sits under the stool and parallel to the sill

artisan: the head or lead carpenter in the 17th, 18th, and 19th centuries

ash: a deciduous tree, or hardwood

base cap: a separate strip of molding that is designed to sit atop the base main board (to create a base molding)

batten and board: a wainscoting pattern where vertical boards are affixed in front of small vertical strips of wood (battens)

beading: curved vertical strips that run between wainscoting boards

bevel: an angle cut at the edge of a flat surface

birch: a deciduous tree, or hardwood

blue painter's tape: having less of an adhesive than traditional masking tape, is used to mask/protect surfaces without damaging the finish on the surface

board and batten: a wainscoting pattern where the vertical strips of wood (battens) are affixed in front of the wider vertical boards

brad: a small finish nail under 1¹/₂" long

butt joint: where a piece of wood cut at 90 degrees sits flush against another piece

cap: a molding that sits atop another; usually refers to the top horizontal trim of the wainscoting

casing, door: the interior molding that runs on the wall surface around the perimeter of a doorway

casing, window: the interior molding that runs on the wall surface around the perimeter of a window opening

cat's-paw: a handle with a hook on the other end resembling the claw end of a hammer, used as an aid in prying wood pieces apart and removing

caulk: soft toothpastelike material, sold in tubes and available in a variety of colors and elements,

used to fill cracks and holes; solidifies after application

caulking gun: holds a tube of caulk with trigger and release to disperse the material

cedar: a coniferous tree, or softwood

chair rail: interior molding run horizontally around the perimeter of the room on the wall surface, usually between 32" and 36" from the floor

chalk line: a mark of chalk on a surface left from the positioning of a chalk line reel in a straight line, used as a measurement/guide

chalk line reel: a tool consisting of a spool of string rolled within a container filled with chalk; used to mark straight lines as a guide/measurement on wood, drywall, or cement surfaces

chamfer: to shave/contour the edge of a wood piece, usually with a plane

chisel: metal tool consisting of handle and blade (tang) used to dig, scrape, and shave portions of wood

combination square: tool used as guide to measure/mark and confirm 90-degree angles; also has level tube for level and/or plumb readings

compass: expanding tool used to mark accurate distances from one point and/or in combination with equal or alternating bisecting distances

compressor: metal container designed to trap air and release the buildup in order to aid in a wide variety of power-tool operations

compressor, pancake: circular, flattened-shaped compressor, usually smaller than other conical-shaped compressors

coniferous: refers to a softwood tree that reproduces by seedlings grouped in a cone and generally has needles instead of leaves

coped joint: wood cut along the profile of a miter cut joined to a piece of the same molding

cure: the time it takes for an applied material to completely *dry;* for oil-based/alkyd paints, and polyurethane it is the point when the solvent has completely oxidized, leaving the other ingredients (additives, binders, pigments) hard; and for water/latex-based paints and caulks it is the point when the solvent (water) has completely evaporated

cut in: complete a painted section by drawing a line along a certain point with the brush

dado: the lower portion of an interior wall; also refers to a groove that is dug, gouged, chiseled, or routed; usually in a straight line

deciduous: refers to a hardwood tree that reproduces usually by seedlings of fruits or nuts and generally has leaves instead of needles

doorjamb: the inside frame of a doorway

drywall: also called Sheetrock and gypsum board, fastened directly onto studs and used for interior walls; comes in thicknesses of 1/4", 1/2", 5/8", and 3/4" and 4' lengths of 8' and 10'

drywall grate: a tool used to shave plaster or drywall down, resembles a cheese grater

end cutters: pliers with sharp pincers on end used for cutting the ends off nails or screws or pulling partially driven nails out

file: metal tool with handle, varying coarseness used for shaping, sanding, smoothing, and scraping

finish nailer: a pneumatic nail gun used with finish nails for moldings

fir, Douglas: a softwood, or coniferous, tree

fireplace surround: the molding and/or stone configuration on the wall surface around the perimeter of a firebox (fireplace)

flat miter: a cut of some degrees made with the molding sitting flat

framer: the rough carpenter responsible for the skeleton and framing of the structure

fur: to bring out a surface by means of some material, such as a shim behind a piece of molding or wood strips placed on top of studs

furring strip: a length of wood installed/ inserted onto a surface

gouge: metal tool of varying shapes (scooped and V) used to dig and shape wood

grinder: a hand-held power tool that is used to wear away a metal, concrete, or wood surface

grit: a measurement used to indicate the level of coarseness of a surface (as in sandpaper, for instance)

hammer, claw: basic hammer with a curved claw for removing nails, about 13" long and most widely used for interior finish carpentry

hammer, framing: larger than a claw hammer, with straight rather than curved claw, comes in sizes beginning with 14" long, used primarily by rough carpenters and framers

hammer, ripping: hammer with straight claw on head, about 13" long and used primarily for interior rough carpentry

hardwood: heavier wood from deciduous or broad-leafed trees (like oak, mahogany, and maple)

header: the horizontal portion at the top of an opening (door, window, or firebox)

hone: to grind, sharpen, or sand

hydroscopic: with moisture moving in and out of wood due to its microscopic honeycomb pattern

index point: meter on a miter saw that is moved manually to re-position blade within housing

interior finisher: the carpenter who works on the inside of the house responsible for installing the cabinetry, stairs, windows, doors, and trim

iron: the metal blade on the plane

jigsaw: slang word used for saber saw or orbital saw; power hand tool specialized in making cuts along a curve

joinery: trim work in and on a structure, also called millwork

joists: supports of a structure that run horizontally and to which the floor and/or ceiling are affixed

kerf: repetitive cut made in a strip of wood (not all the wall through) to allow it to be bent without breaking

knot: a section of the wood where a limb or branch has been sliced through

level: an imaginary line or plane joining two points of equal height

machine oil: lubrication used for tools with metal components to prevent rust

mahogany: a deciduous tree, or hardwood

main board: the central portion of the multiple-piece base molding on which the base cap and/or shoe molding is attached

maple: a deciduous tree, or hardwood

material stand: an adjustable level to rest moldings on; works in conjunction with a saw or another table or stand

MDF: Medium Density Fiberboard

mill: factory where the lumber is precision-cut into planks and moldings

millwork: trim work in and on a structure, also called joinery

millworker: carpenter who makes the doors and door frames, windows and window frames, and interior trim

miter joint: where two pieces of molding, cut on the same degree, attach to form an angle

mitered return: a piece of molding cut at 45 degrees on one side attached to another piece of the same profile cut at 45 degrees from the other

miterless base molding: prefabricated components complete with inside and outside corners designed to be installed with the lengths of base cut only at 90 degrees

miterless crown molding: prefabricated system complete with inside and outside corners designed to be installed with the strips of crown cut only at 90 degrees

molding, base: the interior trim that runs horizontally on the wall at the floor, generally around the perimeter of the room

molding, coronado crown: a popular, easy-to-recognize profile

molding, cove: trim with concave profile

molding, crown: the interior trim that runs horizontally on the wall at the ceiling, generally around the perimeter of a room

molding, picture: trim installed horizontally on wall below ceiling fashioned for hooks/wire to suspend from, attached to framed artwork

molding, shoe: strip of trim installed at foot of base main board

moulding: the archaic (and British) spelling of *molding*

multiple-piece base: a base configuration consisting of two or more molding profiles

multiple-piece crown: a crown configuration consisting of two or more molding profiles

nail set: metal tool used as aid to drive nails down beyond outer surface of wood

oak, white and red: deciduous trees, or hardwoods

oilstone: abrasive flat stone used to hone chisels

one-by: slang referring to dimension of wood that is denoted 1" thick but in reality 3/4" thick

orbital saw: also called a saber saw; power hand tool specialized in making cuts along a curve

outlet receptacle: electric socket or "plug"

panel adhesive: thick glue designed for construction use, generally manufactured in tubes

perpendicular: a line in relation to a dissecting one at 90 degrees

piloted hole: hole drilled as a preparation for nail or screw

pine: a coniferous tree, or softwood

plane, bench: the most commonly used plane, category name for hand planes

plane, block: the smallest (4"–7") and most versatile of the bench planes

plane, bullnose rabbet: small hand plane with blade and throat justified to one side enabling it to shave flush

plane, jack: medium-sized (about 14") bench plane

plane, jointer: the largest (24" long) of the bench planes

plane, molding: large plane used in yesteryear to aid in contouring of wood to profile custom moldings; still available today as an antique

plane, spokeshave: small butterfly-shaped plane used to shave curved edges

plastic junction box: open with sides and back, affixed to a stud or joist, where hot and neutral wiring is run for purpose of hooking up switch, light, outlet receptacle, or other electrical device

plate rail: wide wainscot cap molding with flat grooved surface designed to hold plates in place standing against wall

plinth block: lower portion of column or casing

plumb: an exactly vertical imaginary line

plywood: wood consisting of multiple thin layers glued together with grain of each layer dissecting at different points

plywood, birch shop: layered wood with outer surfaces consisting of birch veneer; most commonly used by cabinetmakers

pneumatic nail gun: a power tool hooked to a compressor that sets nails

polyurethane: a finish coating used for sealing and protecting floors and furniture; generally oil-based and containing plastic resins; usually clear with a slight amber tint

poplar: a deciduous tree, or medium-density hardwood

profile: the cross section of a molding, usually refers to a specific style of trim

proud: carpentry jargon referring to a portion of wood protruding

pry bar: metal tool with curved flattened end, used as a wedge to aid in prying materials apart

PSI: pressure indicator standing for Pounds per Square Inch

pure bristle brush: brush with natural (not manufactured) hair used for solvent-based coatings

putty knife: thin flattened metal tool with handle, blade up to 4" wide

rasp: file with large teeth for coarse finishing

redwood: a coniferous tree, or softwood, readily available in western states

reveal: visible portion of wood underlying another piece

rip cut: cutting a piece of wood against the grain

ripping bar: large flattened metal tool with curved end, used for prying and as a wedge

saber saw: also called an orbital saw; power hand tool specialized in making cuts along a curve

sanding block, flexible: small foam square covered with irregular-shaped gravel meant for sanding surfaces

saw, back-: category of handsaws that cut on the pull back stroke

saw, chop: miter saw with circular (generally 10"–12") blade that can be moved up and down on turntable

saw, circular: hand-held power tool usually with 7¼" blade, also called hypoid and worm drive saw

saw, coping: handsaw with thin blade used to make curved cuts in relatively thin stock and to cut out along the profile of a molding

saw, crosscut: handsaw with small, beveled teeth jutting alternately from side to side, used for rough cuts

saw, flush-cut: fine-toothed handsaw with arm attached at different level from blade to allow close cuts (through casing straight along floor, for instance)

saw, hand-operated miter: portable fence with moving table and block saw for cutting molding at various angles

saw, hypoid: hand-held circular saw, 7 1/4" blade, also called worm drive saw

saw, rip: handsaw with large teeth

saw, saber: power hand tool specialized in making cuts along a curve, also called orbital saw

saw, slide compound miter: chop saw with adjustable blade situated on slide pipes, enabling it to move forward and back on the turntable

saw, trim: hand-held small circular saw, 4 1/2" blade

saw, worm drive: hand-held circular saw, 7 1/4" blade, also called hypoid saw

scarf joint: where two pieces of molding attach to form one continuous piece

scribe: to mark for notation or measurement

shellac: an alcohol-based primer usually used for sealing water stains or knots in new wood; originates as egg-protecting resin of the laccifera insect dissolved in alcohol

shim: to bring out a surface by means of some material, such as a strip placed behind a piece of molding or wood strips placed on top of studs

sill: lower horizontal section situated on the outside of a window frame

softwood: lighter wood from coniferous or needle trees (like pine, redwood, and cedar)

spackle, lightweight: a plasterlike soft material used to fill cracks and holes, dries quicker and with less shrinking than traditional heavier, wetter spackle compounds

stool: lower horizontal section situated on the inside of a window frame

stud finder: tool used to locate position of studs within the walls and joists in the ceiling

T-bevel: adjustable measuring tool used to determine the angle of a corner

tack cloth: fibrous fabric treated with resin for purpose of wiping/cleaning surfaces of dust/dirt particles

tang: metal portion of chisel blade within the handle

throat: the opening in the bottom of the plane through which the blade extends

tongue-in-groove: wood panels designed to interlock together and appear as single pattern

trim out: install finish molding and paneling on an area

try square: measuring tool manufactured with true 90-degree angle

urethane: a water-based finish coating with plastic resins that is used to seal floors and furniture; dries clear and, unlike polyurethane, usually has no amber tint

utility knife: handle holding single-edge blade, used for shaving, cutting, and scribing

vertical miter: a cut of some degrees made with the molding sitting upright against the fence of the saw

vertical projection: the distance from the ceiling that a crown molding (when installed on the wall at the ceiling) will sit on the wall

wainscot cap: molding installed horizontally as trim above wainscot panels

wainscoting: molding and/or paneling covering the dado, or lower portion of the wall, consisting of the base, chair rail or wainscoting cap, and section between

walnut: a deciduous tree, or hardwood

waterstone: abrasive flat stone used to hone chisels

INDEX

NOTES

NOTES

NOTES

NOTES

NOTES

NOTES